SOJOURN

SOJOURN

Karma, Reincarnation, and the Evolution of the Soul

GINA LAKE

Endless Satsang Foundation

Endless Satsang Foundation

www.radicalhappiness.com

Cover photograph: © Andreygorlov/Dreamstime.com

ISBN: 978-1463781187

Copyright © 2011 by Gina Lake

All rights reserved. No part of this book may be used or reproduced by any means, graphic, electronic, or mechanical, including photocopying, recording, taping, or by any information storage retrieval system without the written permission of the publisher except in the case of brief quotations embodied in critical articles and reviews.

CONTENTS

Preface   vii

Introduction   ix

PART 1: The Stages of Evolution

CHAPTER 1: The Journey   1

Reincarnation and Karma—Before the Beginning—The Stages of the Journey—The Stages of Humanity's Journey—Evolution in Other Kingdoms and Realities—The Five Cycles—Physical Development—Emotional Development—Intellectual Development—Spiritual Development

CHAPTER 2: The Journey Begins   19

The Infant Cycle—The Baby Cycle

CHAPTER 3: Youth   37

The Young Cycle

CHAPTER 4: Maturity   47

The Mature Cycle—The Old Cycle—Other Factors That Influence Behavior

CHAPTER 5: Soul Age and Behavior   65

Raising Children—Education—Work—Recreation—Sexuality

CHAPTER 6: Soul Age and Relationships   85

Family Relationships—Romantic Relationships—Other Relationships

PART 2: How Karma Works and Traumas Are Healed

CHAPTER 7: Near Deaths and Traumatic Deaths   101
CHAPTER 8: Traumatic Accidents   115
CHAPTER 9: Murder and Suicide   123
CHAPTER 10: Unfortunate Love Affairs   135
CHAPTER 11: Unfulfilled Potential   145
CHAPTER 12: Slavery and Servitude   151
CHAPTER 13: Mental Illness and Mental Disability   161
CHAPTER 14: Imprisonment and Seclusion   173
CHAPTER 15: Conclusion   183

About the Author   191

PREFACE

The information about soul evolution and the stories of past lives were given to me by my nonphysical teacher. This was written in 1997, and although metaphysics, reincarnation, and karma aren't central to what I'm currently teaching and writing about, I offer this book in hopes that it will lead to more compassion and understanding.

G. L. February, 2009

INTRODUCTION

With telecommunications making the world a global community, it's especially important that we learn to appreciate the diversity of the human population and its cultures. Every day, in the streets, in our businesses, in our classrooms, and on television, we encounter people from different cultures and walks of life. They are our neighbors, our employees, our employers, and our co-workers. Daily, we are challenged to understand each other and appreciate our differences. We need to begin living in greater harmony with each other. The ideas in this book provide a reason for doing that as well as a way for understanding our diversity. They are offered with hope for a better world.

Reincarnation is such an important concept in helping us understand and appreciate our differences. Part One describes the stages of our journey on earth, which take place over many lifetimes, and the impact these stages have on how we live. Each stage in this journey is unique in its perceptions, lessons, and contributions. As we move through each stage, we see life through the lens of that stage and encounter the lessons of those perceptions, which shape them into new perceptions. The reason for learning about these stages is to shed light on the journey and the tasks along the way, not so that we can better compare ourselves with others. A greater understanding of the function and perceptions of each stage can help us relate to each other more compassionately.

Part Two contains teachings about karma, another important concept in understanding life. Part Two shows how our soul operates throughout our many lifetimes to deliver our lessons and heal our psychological wounds, which often prevent us from fulfilling our potentials and experiencing our spiritual nature. These teachings are in the form of stories that show how karma has worked in the lives of real people. These stories also illustrate how unique every situation is.

These stories were obtained through clairaudience, or channeling. This phenomenon has existed throughout history and is one way that knowledge is introduced into the world. Of course, you're free to reject any of this information. But I think even the most skeptical of minds will enjoy reading the accounts and examining their logic.

My hope in writing this is that your sojourn on earth will be made a little easier because of the light this information sheds on the human dilemma. We are travelers enmeshed now in our own perceptions of life. But at the end, we will see that it has all been a fine journey in which we have been not only the actors, but also the originators of the story. May this serve you as a roadmap.

PART 1

The Stages of Evolution

CHAPTER 1
The Journey

REINCARNATION AND KARMA

Reincarnation is the belief that we live many lifetimes in many different bodies with a period of review, reflection, and growth in between lifetimes. Reincarnation supposes that we are spirit, or a soul, traveling through the world of matter, which is like a school for us. The lessons of the physical universe are many and so demand many different bodies. A variety of bodies allows our soul to experience a variety of times, environments, people, cultures, and challenges. A variety of bodies also allows us to experience life through the ever-changing lens of our evolutionary status. So a young soul will learn something different from a situation than an old soul in the same situation. So not only do our circumstances change in each of our lifetimes, but also what we bring to those circumstances changes and so our experience of those circumstances is different.

You may be wondering why we bother—why do we have to experience all this pain and struggle? The answer to this can't be fully appreciated from the physical frame of reference. But once we're out of the body, why we bother is eminently clear: We choose to. Our soul—the spark of the Divine within us—eagerly embraces *all* experience and the opportunities those experiences afford for growth. When we quiet ourselves long enough in meditation to experience our divine Self, we know this. We know our existence to be purposeful—and glorious.

Contrary to what many think about reincarnation, we are not on an endless treadmill or wheel, returning to life to make amends, only to reincarnate again in another imperfect form. No, we are here to evolve beyond the physical plane. For that, perfection is not required, since human beings can never be perfect. For that, only understanding and love are required. When we have finished with the lessons of the physical plane, we move on to another plane and its lessons. Just as certain lessons can only be learned on the physical plane, others can only be learned on other planes, which aren't physical at all. Life is a progression: The wisdom gained in one lifetime is carried into the next and built upon. This continues indefinitely on other planes as well.

We are continually evolving, as is the Divine, of which we are an expression. We are not entities apart from our creator as much as aspects of the Creator, which continually expand it. We don't have to become God—we already are God (or an expression of God)! This explanation is simplistic, but useful. It may be all we can hope to grasp of our greatness while in the physical body and limited by the mind and senses.

Like reincarnation, the concept of karma is often misunderstood. Some people think that their problems are punishment for something they did in a former lifetime. This couldn't be farther from the truth or the spirit of karma. Karma is the means by which we receive the lessons we need to evolve and return Home, to our true nature. Our karma is the situation created to teach us these lessons.

These teachings come in many forms, some painful and some not. Actually, many of our challenges aren't karmic at all, but chosen by our souls to speed our growth. Challenges are the means by which we evolve and become conscious of ourselves as divine, as something beyond our personal self—not proof that we did something wrong in a former lifetime. Difficulties are part of the natural process of evolution on the physical plane.

The nature of life is to evolve, and this sometimes necessitates pain. Blaming ourselves, others, or God for our misfortunes is a waste of energy and a misuse of our will. And yet, we're free to choose blame over acceptance, even though this will lead to stagnation and pain rather than wisdom. Although we may not be able to choose whether or not we will evolve (we all eventually do), we do choose *how* we'll evolve—slowly or quickly, through pain or through acceptance. Accepting everything that comes to us is the joyful choice.

Karma is an impartial and wise teacher. Furthermore, we participate in choosing our karmic circumstances. They are chosen through a cooperative decision-making process entered into willingly by the souls involved, not meted out by an external judge. We choose the circumstances that will teach us to make better choices. Life is an exercise in free will, not only when we are incarnate, but also before entering the body.

BEFORE THE BEGINNING

To appreciate the purpose of life on the physical plane, it might be helpful to try to understand the state we existed in before our incarnations on earth. Although I don't presume to know our origins, the following myth is one conception of the story of Life, which shares many similarities with other creation stories from all over the world:

> *In the beginning was darkness and the Void. The Creator existed as undifferentiated energy, infinite and all-inclusive. Then, the Light was born and shined upon the Void. With the Light, came awareness of being, and the Creator smiled. This gave rise to an urge to further differentiate and explore that which is differentiated. And so the physical universes were born. The Creator breathed life into them by sending a portion of itself into matter. This way, it could experience life through the perspective of matter. Each new experience fueled the Creator's desire for further experience and differentiation.*
>
> *While incarnate, we, as part of creation, are connected to the Creator and long for the unity we have lost. This desire to reunite with the Creator, to return to the primeval state of Oneness, is the energy that fuels evolution. When evolution is complete, the Creator recalls that portion of itself back unto itself and sends forth others. The energy of creation is constantly in motion, moving from unity with the Creator to enmeshment in its creations and back again to unity. In and out of creation, the creative energy moves, all the while expanding the Creator's understanding and love.*

This is an allegory and shouldn't be taken too literally. The fact is that when we are in a body, we aren't capable of fully grasping the truth of who we are and our origin. But this shouldn't and doesn't prevent most of us from trying to understand our origins and purpose for being here. And, fortunately, there does come a time when our intellectualizations about this are overshadowed by the experience of our true nature. When this happens, we know we aren't far from Home.

As the myth describes, the Creator differentiates and sends a portion of itself into the myriad physical forms on our plane to experience this plane's diverse possibilities. The Creator breathes life, or a portion of itself, into matter. This life expresses itself on many different levels: human, animal, plant, and mineral. These are the various kingdoms of matter. But of them all, humankind and possibly the cetaceans (whales and dolphins) stand alone in their ability to contemplate their reality, think rationally, make choices, and learn from those choices.

THE STAGES OF THE JOURNEY

Ever since human beings incarnated and forgot their divine origins, they have wondered who they are and why they are here. The answer to this is different for each stage of our sojourn on earth and reflects the various states of consciousness along the way. By investigating how people at each stage answer this question, we get a glimpse of how they see the world and their place in it.

In some ways, those in the first stage of evolution are closer to their divine nature than some older souls because they are so fresh from the original state of unity. Unlike older souls, they still see themselves as part of the universe rather than separate from it. The term used to describe this state of non-differentiation in primitive humankind is *animistic*. This state is similar to that of the human infant who perceives the mother and father and everything that comes into its life as part of itself.

In this state in primitive humankind, the sense of oneness is not all-encompassing, but one of oneness with nature and the family group or tribe. It's not the oneness experienced at the end of our evolutionary journey, when there's little question about who we are and why we are here. Animism eventually dissolves with each succeeding lifetime as the ego is strengthened.

By the time we have reached the stage beyond animism, corresponding to youth, we are enmeshed in the personality and its ruler, the ego. This stage represents the height of separation. Just as youths struggle to differentiate themselves from their parents and establish their own identity, those at this stage seek to develop themselves as separate and powerful entities. In this stage, we see ourselves as the center of the universe and in conflict with others. This stage develops the ego to its fullest.

After this stage, in the stage of maturity, the ego's grip begins to loosen. The answer to the question, "Who am I?" broadens, as we begin to identify ourselves not only with loved ones, but also with humanity in general. At this stage, the question, "Why am I here?" becomes pressing, as we seek meaning that goes beyond the ego's goals. This questioning continues into the final stage where, at last, some answers are found. In the final stage, we begin to glimpse our divine nature and understand the divine plan.

THE STAGES IN HUMANITY'S JOURNEY

We as individuals are making this journey, but humanity as a whole is also passing through these stages. There was a time when most people on earth were in the earliest stage of evolution. Then, animism was the representative state of consciousness and humanity's religions reflected that. The gods were assumed to be actively involved in their lives and present in the forms of nature.

People at this stage developed elaborate rituals that helped them feel they had some power to control their destinies. But they saw their power as coming from the gods and not from within themselves. In this stage of evolution, feelings of powerlessness and dependency on supernatural forces presided. Nevertheless, early human beings learned to survive in their unpredictable and dangerous world, and they developed a philosophy that helped them cope with their feelings of powerlessness and fear. Religion provided comfort and an explanation for the unpredictable and seemingly cruel events of life.

The next step in humankind's evolutionary journey was out of animism and into a worldview that saw human beings as children of an anthropomorphic god. This god passed judgment on them and either damned them to hell or sent them to a blissful paradise. This is a familiar perspective even today because, although many have evolved beyond this stage, many are still at this stage.

Feelings of powerlessness and fear continue to pervade this worldview, and the previous stage's animistic sense of oneness is replaced by a sense of separation. At this stage, the world is seen in polarities: us vs. them, God vs. Man, good vs. evil. In this worldview, there is no room for the shades of gray, which are so much a part of the perception of later stages. The religions of this second stage reflect this philosophy, as does the hierarchy in their governments, families, and businesses.

This polarized and hierarchical mentality carries over somewhat into the next stage of evolution, the stage to which most of the world's people have now evolved. This is the stage corresponding to youth in humanity's evolution. The difference between this stage and the last is that those at this stage rely more on themselves and less on authority. The individual acts as his or her own authority and tries to be an authority to others.

In this stage, the ego is king and power is sought for one's own benefit rather than for the benefit of one's tribe or one's God. Those at this stage today have built a highly technological society capable of fulfilling every physical comfort and ego desire. But their sense of separation and their competition with the environment and desire for power and comfort have brought humanity to a critical point, which is forcing us to reevaluate our relationship to life and to each other.

The next stage in the evolution of humankind corresponds to maturity, or adulthood, and is yet to come. When this time does arrive, it will change the tone of life on this planet significantly. Those at this stage have a greater sensitivity to the plight of others, a longing for the Divine, and more resources and talents to put to use to improve conditions on earth. The world at this stage will be a very different place.

The last stage, when most people on earth would be in the final stage of their evolution, is hard to imagine. It will be one in which brotherhood and the Divine will be honored above all else and most of our physical needs will be easily met. This will leave us free to explore our talents and experience life from the perspective of our true nature rather than from the perspective of the ego.

The names that will be used to describe these stages of human evolution are the names given to these stages in the book *Messages from Michael* by Chelsea Quinn Yarbro: the Infant cycle, the Baby cycle, the Young cycle, the Mature cycle, and the Old cycle. These five stages, or cycles, will be the framework used to discuss the evolution of human consciousness and its lessons.

People in each cycle have their own way of perceiving life, which is why understanding each other is so hard. Furthermore, we can only understand and accept different perspectives if we have experienced those perspectives ourselves. The purpose of examining these differences is not to figure out who is more evolved, but to bring greater understanding, compassion, and patience to human relations. Hopefully, this information will not be used to judge others. Even so, it's too important not to consider.

Our sojourn on earth begins with the first breath of the first incarnation in the Infant cycle and ends with the last breath of our last incarnation in the Old cycle. Because it takes many, many lifetimes in each cycle to learn the lessons of that cycle, most people have lived hundreds of lifetimes before reincarnation on earth is done. The number of lifetimes it takes to complete the journey depends on how fast we progress through the lessons and how many resting lifetimes we choose. We all choose some resting lifetimes for recuperation, which do little to advance our progress.

As an aside, it might be important to mention that some people who are alive today have already evolved beyond earth and have come here from other dimensions to help during this critical time on earth. Many of these individuals are here for only one lifetime, and they bring advanced consciousness, intelligence, and talents to this world.

EVOLUTION IN OTHER KINGDOMS AND REALITIES

Evolution on earth is distinct from evolution in other physical realities, although there are threads of similarity in all physical systems. The most basic similarity is that every physical system has unconditional love as its goal. Another similarity is that all physical systems evolve by means of trial and error, that is, the process of evolution is the same in every physical system. Some of the lessons are the same as well. But because of the vast diversity in the universe, lessons in one system may bear no resemblance to lessons in another.

For instance, where individuals are without emotional bodies, lessons pertaining to the emotions are irrelevant. But emotional development is central to our evolution because, in our system, developing unconditional love is related to emotional development. In other systems, unconditional love might be developed by other means. The universe is infinite and anything we can imagine exists. With this in mind, let's focus on our particular system and its characteristics and lessons.

THE FIVE CYCLES

We are body, mind, emotions, and spirit. In each of these areas, we meet lessons, but certain lessons are more important in some cycles than in others. What we learn in each cycle is stored in our unconscious to be used and built on in later cycles. The lessons encountered in our earliest lifetimes pertain primarily to physical survival. Once these are learned, which takes many lifetimes, we focus on emotional and intellectual growth and then on developing specific skills and talents. In our final lifetimes, spiritual development becomes the goal, as we are ready to experience our true nature and begin expressing that in the world more.

How many lifetimes are spent learning each lesson depends on several things, particularly on our willingness to learn from our mistakes. We are free to accept or reject advice from others and make other choices that will either enhance or diminish our ability to learn our lessons. Another factor in how quickly we learn our lessons is the amount and kind of learning that has taken place in previous lifetimes. Conclusions we have drawn about our experiences in former lifetimes subconsciously influence our perceptions and how easily we accept new learning. Another factor is our personality. Everyone is born with inclinations and tendencies, determined by his or her astrology chart and other esoteric factors.

To understand the journey better, it might be helpful to outline the evolution of the physical, emotional, intellectual, and spiritual dimensions of our being.

PHYSICAL DEVELOPMENT

The first lessons pertain to maintaining the physical body. The physical lessons are central to our earliest lifetimes because they teach us how to obtain the food, water, shelter, sleep, and warmth we need to survive. In the early stages of our evolution, life provides experiences that teach us the value of hard work perseverance, patience, endurance, responsibility, caution, realism, and practicality. Failure to develop these qualities in response to the challenges of life leads to death or a significant decrease in comfort and security. The reward for learning these lessons is being able to deal effectively with the world and provide for our basic needs.

Once some basic survival skills are achieved, usually somewhere in the Young cycle, some choose to continue developing their physical abilities, although no one is required to. Like other talents, physical talents, such as athletic prowess, eye-hand coordination, agility, and manual dexterity take lifetimes to develop, but the drive to develop these talents shows up earlier than for most other talents. This shouldn't be surprising, given that the Young cycle is a time for ego development, and ego development is more related to developing the physical body and its skills and the attainment of material security than to other talents, such as musical or artistic ability.

EMOTIONAL DEVELOPMENT

Because emotional development is intrinsic to developing unconditional love, the emotional lessons also begin early in our incarnations. For the same reason, emotional development continues to be important in each cycle, with each cycle having its emotional challenges and characteristic expression of feelings.

Fear is the overriding emotion of the Infant cycle. Because the youngest souls live in fear of nearly everything, venturing out into the world is threatening and avoided whenever possible. When Infant souls are confronted or feel threatened, they either withdraw or lash out angrily or even violently, depending on the degree to which they feel threatened. Their anger is automatic, uncontrolled, and primitively expressed. And because their egos are tenuous and their coping mechanisms are undeveloped, these youngest souls are easily overwhelmed by life. This often leads to a life of isolation or dependency on those willing to shield the Infant soul from the threatening forces in the world.

The degree of love that Infant souls are capable of feeling is limited. What love and joy they do experience is usually closer to appreciation than love as most of us know it. So if their protectors fail to shield them or abdicate this responsibility, Infant souls are no longer likely to feel love, but hatred and revenge. For the youngest souls, there is a fine line between love and hate. Consequently, violence is common in families with very young souls.

The Baby soul's emotional range is more extensive than the Infant soul's, although Baby souls' emotional reactions remain primitive. Fear and anger are still profoundly felt. But the most distinctive feature of emotional development in the Baby cycle is the appearance of guilt and shame. A degree of conscience develops by the Baby cycle that allows guilt and shame to come into play. Jealousy is another feeling activated in the Baby cycle because attachments to others have developed. While the Infant soul's experience of love was one of dependency, the Baby soul's is one of possession. Baby souls are a little more able to understand and respond to the feelings of others than Infant souls, but sensitivity and compassion are still at a very elementary level.

In the Young cycle, emotional expression is similar in many ways to that of the Baby cycle, but fear is less prevalent, and anger and aggression are more so. Young souls see themselves as separate from others and have learned to respond aggressively to the environment rather than passively. This is an important step in their emotional development, but Young souls need to learn to control or channel their aggressive impulses. For most, this isn't achieved until well into the Mature cycle. So for much of the Young cycle, Young souls expend their energy aggressively defending themselves and then coping with the problems caused by that in their relationships. For this and other reasons, relationships are a major area of learning for them.

Although Young souls have a greater capacity to love than Baby or Infant souls, to them, love means possessing people and trying to get them to fulfill their needs. The lover is an object of gratification and a source of security for the Young soul. But that is fine. At least these feelings bond them with people long enough to develop some genuine feelings of camaraderie. For Young souls, love is a "you and me against the world" proposition but a necessary step along the road to learning to love more deeply.

Rather than blaming others for their problems, as in the Young cycle, Mature souls try to understand others and are more willing to accept their share of the responsibility for any problems. This shift from childlike egocentricity to adult self awareness and self responsibility is a major step in emotional development. Mature souls have also learned to cope better with their fears and to control their anger, often through repression.

In the Mature cycle, self blame and self denial replace the dogmatism and self-centeredness of the earlier cycles. Anxiety, discontent, apathy, alienation, boredom, depression, and confusion make this a difficult cycle. Mature souls are all too aware of the differences between themselves and others, resulting in continual self-questioning and seeking. This is often ameliorated through psychological counseling or a humanistic philosophy.

The ability to love has strengthened greatly by the Mature cycle, and many Mature souls find partners with whom they are comfortable and happy for life. Problems with trust, jealousy, and the usual challenges of personal love remain, but Mature souls are more in command of these feelings than in former cycles. This may be because they are more able to be objective about their behavior and the behavior of others. This is the cycle in which the most emotional growth takes place, probably because the emotional discomfort of this stage challenges us to move beyond our old ways of responding.

The emotional challenges of the Mature cycle continue somewhat into the Old cycle, but the emotions present less of a problem as we progress through this cycle. Fear, anger, jealousy, and other negative emotions are supplanted by peace, love, joy, and acceptance as this cycle progresses. Old souls know how to detach from their negative emotions and use them as guides. This doesn't mean they don't have bouts with depression, but depression is less frequent and more manageable than in the Mature cycle. The depression they do have is more apt to be produced by disillusionment with the material world and by their desire to return Home than by not being able to obtain material satisfaction.

Love as Old souls know it is closer to unconditional love, although this is an ideal and rarely a constant in anyone's life. So love becomes more inclusive and more impersonal in this cycle, extending even to so-called enemies. Old souls are often able to see beyond the personality of even their enemies, recognizing the Divine in them and their oneness with them.

INTELLECTUAL DEVELOPMENT

Intellectual ability is not a function of our level of evolution except beyond a certain level. Everyone, regardless of soul age, has a certain capacity to think, although the later cycles are often used to develop the intellect more fully. However, objectivity, or the ability to separate our thoughts from our feelings, is a function of our level of evolution. The achievement of objectivity is a major goal of intellectual development, and not until the late Young cycle is some degree of objectivity attained.

The Infant cycle is less concerned with intellectual development than with survival. Little energy is spent developing the intellect unless survival is dependent on it.

During the Baby cycle, improving communication with others, particularly about needs, is the primary intellectual concern. Improved communication helps Baby souls accomplish their goals of survival and mutual dependency. In this cycle, intellectual interests are still narrow, with little interest in anything that doesn't immediately affect them and their safety and comfort.

In the Young cycle, the intellect is primarily developed in the pursuit of the Young soul's goals. The experiences of the Young cycle demand a certain level of intellect, and the intellect will be exercised in meeting these demands. But not until the Mature cycle do we begin to apply our intellect to specific tasks that develop it in exceptional ways.

The greatest intellectual development occurs in the Mature cycle. At some point in this cycle, most of the basic lessons have been learned and more time is spent focused on specific life purposes, many of which require a high level of intellect. When that is the case, intellectual development may be the main focus for many lifetimes. But not every Mature soul takes on life purposes that demand extensive intellectual development. For those who don't, the Mature cycle may not be intellectually focused at all. Intellectual development beyond a certain level is a choice, not a requirement.

Intellectual development in the Old cycle is a continuation of previous development. If the individual has been involved in life purposes requiring complex intellectual abilities, these abilities will continue to be strengthened. But if the individual's tasks don't require intellectual prowess, the Old cycle may hardly focus on these abilities at all. Of course, our intellectual abilities are strengthened just by living. So even an Old soul who isn't intellectually inclined may function better intellectually than an early Mature soul.

SPIRITUAL DEVELOPMENT

Every experience we gave is part of our spiritual development, but during the Old cycle, our spiritual development takes on a special significance. It entails developing a philosophy, gaining wisdom and compassion, expressing our love for humanity through service, and developing extrasensory abilities. But more than this, it entails experiencing our divine Self. We are able to experience our true nature more in this cycle than ever before. Until the Old cycle, experiences of ego-transcendence are rare and limited. In the Old cycle, they become increasingly common. By the end of the Old cycle, the personality is clearly recognized as a vehicle for soul development.

Each step of the journey is of equal importance to the attainment of the goal of unconditional love. The next chapters look more closely at each step along the way.

CHAPTER 2
The Journey Begins

THE INFANT CYCLE

When we are first born into physical existence, we are innocent and naive about the ways of the world. As newborn, or Infant, souls, we are like the newborn human infant, incapable of meeting our own needs and coping with the frustration of not having them met. Because there are so few newborn souls in the world today, they are not in most people's experience. Most Infant souls live in remote areas of the globe, where they are nurtured and protected from modern society by their extended families or tribes. So the ordinary person may never encounter even one of these youngest of souls.

The Infant cycle and the succeeding one, the Baby cycle, are the most similar of all the cycles. The basic life lessons are the focus of these two cycles, with survival and the physical lessons being the main focus. Infant souls and, to a lesser extent, Baby souls have the distinction of being closer to the Tao, the state of unity from which we all come, than others on the journey. Even Old souls, except those with only a few lifetimes remaining, are not as identified with the Tao as Infant and Baby souls. This is undoubtedly one reason that life can be so hard for them. Everything is new, and considerable learning needs to take place before even the most basic level of functioning is mastered.

The Infant cycle can best be understood by comparing it to babyhood. Like human infants, Infant souls can't provide for their own needs, and they lack physical coordination. They appear awkward, clumsy, and not fully present in their bodies. Furthermore, the speed with which their sensory input is translated is slow, which makes them seem dull or unintelligent, even though they aren't in most cases. Just as people used to assume that children couldn't understand as much as they can because of their lack of physical skill and ability to communicate, Infant souls are often thought to be mentally deficient.

Another similarity between Infant souls and human infants is their narrow range of emotions. Like human infants, whose basic emotional response is crying, Infant souls respond to the frustrations of life with tears, whining, pouting, whimpering, and resignation. Such primitive emotional reactions contribute to the perception that these individuals are mentally lacking.

Infant souls haven't learned to identify their needs, much less express them sophisticatedly. All they know is that they are scared or uncomfortable, and they respond by demanding comfort and support from those around them. One of the ironies of this is that, because they seem mentally deficient, others often take care of them in ways that interfere with their gaining competency and independence. The best way to help them is to teach them to be more self sufficient. This stage in human evolution requires a delicate balance between offering support and encouraging independence.

Another similarity between human infants and Infant souls is their lack of empathy. Infant souls are notoriously insensitive to the feelings of others. This is not because Infant souls are cruel and want to hurt others, but because, like human infants, Infant souls are incapable of "walking in another's shoes," as the saying goes. Moving beyond egocentricity takes many lifetimes. The only way this is accomplished is by experiencing some of the many different roles in life.

Infant souls may seem to have an incredibly hard task because they have so few resources with which to cope in this challenging world. Life *is* more difficult in the early cycles in terms of survival. The Old cycle is undeniably the easiest one, for even though Old souls sometimes choose challenging lifetimes to accelerate their evolution, they have the resources to cope with them. On the other hand, more mature souls have a greater attachment to physical life and so take it more seriously. That's why, in terms of psychic and emotional pain, the Mature cycle is the most difficult.

So the saving grace for Infant and Baby souls may be that they aren't as attached to life in the physical body as some. This means that when Infant and Baby souls fail, which happens frequently, it matters less to them. They are content to live simple lives in which ego-gratification is limited. This changes dramatically in the Young cycle, when ego-gratification becomes the driving force in life, and remains strong until well into the Old cycle. So although the Infant and Baby cycles are the most difficult, the difficulties don't create the degree of emotional pain that they do in the Young and Mature cycles.

The desire to be in a physical body can be tenuous for Infant souls. They aren't sure they want to stay once they've arrived. The soul is not ambivalent about life, of course. But the personal consciousness may feel so much fear and inadequacy that the desire to escape life is overwhelming. The Infant soul's most common means of escaping life are drugs or alcohol, mental illness, withdrawal, and suicide.

Many Infant souls live numerous short lifetimes before they commit themselves to staying in the body to face their lessons. Given this, it's not surprising that many end up in mental institutions or on the streets (if they were born into a more developed society), or living as hermits. Those in mental institutions display various kinds of mental illness, while some are perfectly sane, although mentally and emotionally incompetent.

Schizophrenia is the mental illness that is most familiar to Infant souls. This by no means implies that all, or even most, schizophrenics are Infant souls. Disassociating themselves from reality and their emotions, as happens in schizophrenia, is one way Infant souls cope with the pain and stimuli of reality. Disassociation allows them to live an insulated life within their own thoughts and delusions and, in some cases, within an institution in which their basic needs are met.

We may have difficulty understanding how anyone would find dissociation and institutionalization more comfortable than reality. In fact, it's not comfortable and it's not a choice in the way that mental illness is a choice for some. It's a deteriorated state that some Infant souls find themselves in when all the coping mechanisms in their tiny repertoire have failed.

Psychosis is also common in Infant souls, occurring for the same reason that schizophrenia occurs. Psychosis has the advantage of some lucid periods between the psychotic outbreaks during which learning can occur. This isn't true of schizophrenia. When schizophrenia is severe enough and left untreated by drugs, schizophrenics are unable to learn life's basic lessons. Fortunately, drugs can prevent the involuntary escape that occurs in schizophrenia and psychosis, so drug treatment can be of real benefit to Infant souls and others.

Infant souls are often involved heavily in drugs and alcohol. Drugs are not only a problem in developed nations. In undeveloped nations, where most Infant souls live, many chew on cocoa leaves, smoke marijuana, ingest peyote and other hallucinogens, or smoke opium as part of their daily life. Those who do this are by no means only Infant souls, but some are. Infant souls find comfort in drugs for many reasons. Drugs help Infant souls forget the pain of reality and the discomfort of their fears; give them a sense of power, which they don't ordinarily have; and provide sensual pleasure, which helps them endure life.

Drugs are one of the easiest and most fleeting routes to temporal happiness, but drug addiction creates more problems than it solves. When the drugs wear off, reality is all the more demanding and confused. Some engage in lifetimes of drug abuse before they realize its fruitlessness. Once this is learned, drugs are no longer likely to be a problem, although other factors, such as the astrology chart and the environment, may play a part in reigniting that desire.

Leading a reclusive lifestyle is the least damaging way that Infant souls cope with their fear. Since those who seclude themselves still have to provide for themselves, they're forced to develop survival skills. But seclusion does nothing for the Infant soul's relationship skills. Infant souls who have had one satisfactory reclusive lifetime often choose a series of them. If this continues too long, a deficit in social and emotional skills may result. Consequently, social lifetimes usually follow reclusive ones. This pattern of reclusive early lifetimes followed by social ones is common and often beneficial for Infant souls because it develops ego strength without overwhelming the Infant soul with emotional and social matters.

The final escape is suicide or, in some cases, self neglect to the point of death. Sometimes when the demands of reality are too difficult and the resources for coping with them too scarce, Infant souls end their lives. Although the soul tries to arrange for support in the Infant soul's environment so that he or she doesn't reach this point, Infant souls often end their lives because they can't see any other way to find peace. This is one reason for putting Infant souls into a structured and moralistic environment, one that encourages them to find other ways of coping with life than suicide. Without this, they may see little reason not to kill or neglect themselves, especially since they live so much in the moment and so little in the consequences of their actions.

Sometimes the inexperience of Infant souls gets them into trouble with the law. They get into trouble because they lack foresight about the consequences of their actions. They are like infants or children in this respect as well. They are both impulsive and oriented toward immediate gratification, yet unable to foresee or appreciate the consequences of their actions. Experience teaches us about consequences, and Infant souls have little or no experience with life. As a result, Infant souls often meet with dramatic consequences.

As for a conscience, Infant souls have one, but it's not very developed yet. The degree to which an Infant soul's conscience functions depends largely on early conditioning. If those around an Infant soul lack morals, then he or she may not develop a conscience. This wouldn't be true of an older soul, who has already developed one in other lifetimes. Consequently, the soul usually places Infant souls in the care of those who will provide moral training and act as positive role models. Sometimes Infant souls are even put in homes that are rigidly moralistic because the simpler, more literal religions suit the Infant soul's need for structure and discipline.

Another characteristic that distinguishes Infant souls from others is their contentment with simple tasks. Farming, cooking, cleaning, sewing, weaving, and other household tasks appeal to them. Although Infant souls aren't mentally deficient as a rule, these tasks are enough for them to handle. Remember that they are just learning to use their bodies and minds. Infant souls have to start with the basics.

This is one reason Infant souls live in parts of the world that have simple social structures and little technology, where they are rarely challenged to do more than they're capable of. The earliest incarnations of the Infant cycle are invariably in rural or undeveloped areas of the world, although later lifetimes in this cycle may be spent in more developed parts of the globe.

Relationships for Infant souls are a one way street, as they are for human infants. They don't know how to give to others yet, but they will learn by being nurtured. The Infant cycle is a time for us to have our needs met by others and rarely a time in which we meet our own needs, much less the needs of others. Our capacity to give is strengthened by these early lifetimes of being cared for by others.

Any relationship in which Infant souls are involved is bound to be a dependent one. This is true even when Infant souls become parents. Infant souls are as incapable of caring for children as any child would be. When they have children, abuse or neglect is common. But children who choose Infant souls as mothers or fathers are rarely Infant souls themselves. They are likely to be Young souls or older, with a foundation of positive nurturing from previous lifetimes. Many who choose Infant soul parents do so to develop compassion that will later enhance their ability to serve others. When a child is placed in a potentially abusive situation, it is almost always by choice and not a karmic requirement.

In love relationships, Infant souls are equally dependent and immature. Their inability to empathize and foresee the consequences of their actions dooms their relationships to difficulties. Furthermore, they expect to be taken care of without giving much in return, making a healthy relationship impossible. As a result, their love relationships are fraught with unrealistic expectations, jealousy, despair, disagreements, and sometimes violence. To aggravate the problem, their partners are usually other very young souls, and neither is capable of setting an example of mature behavior or the give and take necessary for a happy relationship.

The only way out of these difficult relationships is to evolve out of them because any relationship between immature souls is likely to be difficult. So in this stage, it's not so much a question of finding the right partner, but of staying in any relationship long enough to grow up emotionally. Knowing that failure eventually leads to success may be little comfort, yet this is a fact of life, especially in the early stages of evolution.

Peer relationships are equally difficult for Infant souls, who view others as means to an end. With their meager intellectual, social, and emotional resources, Infant souls often rely on manipulation to get what they want. They can become quite adept at this unless others refuse to be manipulated. It takes two to play that game. Infant souls turn to manipulation to get their needs met not only because they lack more skillful means, but also because they lack the self-discipline for achieving what they want. Eventually they learn discipline because they're forced to develop it by circumstances and people along the way. Without a push from circumstances and others, Infant souls might be tempted to continue their pattern of passivity and manipulation.

Self-discipline and many other virtues, such as patience, endurance, and responsibility, are learned early in our evolution out of necessity. These virtues result from mastering the physical lessons, or the lessons most basic to our survival, which are the lessons of the element of earth (in astrological terms). These are the first lessons to be learned. The physical lessons aren't mastered in the Infant or even in the Baby cycle but sometime late in the Young cycle, so the degree of mastery attained in the Infant cycle is elementary.

Infant souls struggle particularly hard with the physical lessons. Their pain comes more from a lack of mastery of these lessons than from their difficulties with relationships. Infant souls don't find relationship issues nearly as distressing—or pressing—as their lack of mastery of the physical lessons, which undermines their ability to survive and augments their fear. They often avoid relationships of all kinds except dependent ones because they find them much too demanding at a time when survival and learning basic tasks are so crucial. Until the physical lessons are learned, survival is difficult and requires most of the Infant soul's energy.

Infant souls learn from the school of hard knocks. This is necessary at this stage of evolution because Infant souls are unable to project themselves or their actions into the future. Until they have acquired some experience, they aren't able to learn vicariously, as older souls do. They first need a background for understanding information from books and others. As a result, in this cycle, learning is more synonymous with pain than in any other cycle.

THE BABY CYCLE

Because this cycle is much like the previous one, much of what has been said about the Infant cycle continues to be true in this one. The main difference between the Infant cycle and this one is the Baby cycle's greater involvement in the emotional aspect of life. Infant souls don't particularly value or seek satisfaction of their emotional needs, nor do they perceive relationships as enhancing their chances for survival. In contrast, Baby souls place as high a value on emotional security and satisfaction as they do on survival, and they see their relationships as significantly contributing to their survival. Baby souls want emotional sustenance from others as well as physical support.

The dependency of the Infant cycle developed attachments to others, which in the Baby cycle extend beyond dependent relationships to other kinds of relationships. The dependency of the Infant cycle also taught the value of nurturing others and fostered a desire to care for others, which comes to fruition in the Baby cycle. We learn to give to others by receiving love and care as infants, and this is no less true for Infant souls. During the Baby cycle, we learn to care both emotionally and physically for others.

Although the desire to care for others is born in the Baby cycle, Baby souls are novices at loving and caring for others. They first have to learn how. To them, loving people means controlling them. In the Baby cycle, feelings of love are self-centered and colored with the conviction that the Baby soul knows what's best for everyone else. Eventually, we realize our loved ones have to find their own way and that loving them means allowing them to do that, but this advance in understanding usually doesn't occur until well into the Mature cycle. Until then, considerable energy goes into trying to control others. This tendency pervades all of the Baby soul's relationships.

Those in the Baby soul's life struggle to make their need for autonomy recognized, but usually to little avail. Baby souls are destined to have relationships that are full of conflict because they're unwilling to allow their loved ones the freedom to explore life in their own way. It's ironic that such young souls think they know what's best for others. This makes more sense when we understand that Baby souls are comparable to two year-olds in human development. Baby souls are as self-centered and headstrong as two year-olds, and Baby souls share feelings of invincibility with two year-olds as well. Baby souls, like two year-olds, are ignorant of the complexities of life, resulting in an unfounded confidence in their own perceptions.

The egocentricity of Baby souls is responsible for their belief that their perceptions are the same as everyone else's and that what's right for them is right for everyone else. Baby souls are narrow minded, opinionated, shortsighted, and stubborn. Moreover, they feel compelled to convert others to their views. As a result, they often find themselves in conflict with those around them.

It's not surprising, then, that Baby souls tend to congregate in small towns or communities of like-minded people. When surrounded by those with similar opinions, Baby souls feel less need to proselytize or convert. "Different is not good" could be their motto. Their lack of understanding about human differences causes them to conclude that they're right and everyone who's different is wrong. In truth, no one is right or wrong, but we don't realize this until we're well beyond the Baby cycle. The polarization created by their strong opinions eventually leads Baby souls to greater acceptance by forcing them to confront new ideas.

The capacity of Baby souls to love is limited by not being able to accept others and their differing perceptions. Baby souls have the most difficulty loving Mature souls because the perceptions of Mature souls are most unlike the Baby soul's. On the other hand, Baby souls feel some compassion and understanding for Infant and other Baby souls because Baby souls have had experience with these stages themselves.

As a result of their relationships with Infant and other Baby souls, Baby souls begin to experience compassion. Consequently, Infant souls are often given to Baby souls to care for as a way of developing the Baby soul's capacity to love. This works because it's easier for Baby souls to love someone who's defenseless and needy than someone who's a potential threat.

Baby souls' ability to love is also limited by a lack of awareness of their feelings and poor communication skills, which are hindrances to getting their needs met within a relationship. Baby souls have little awareness of their needs until those needs cause discomfort for them. By that time, Baby souls usually react angrily and blame others for not meeting their needs rather than discuss those needs. Any feelings of love they might have are often blocked by anger and blame, making it hard for others to respond lovingly to them. At the crux of the interpersonal difficulties of Baby souls is their inability to accept responsibility for their feelings and communicate them. Until this is overcome, their ability to form satisfying relationships is limited.

Even when they are able to manage their anger, Baby souls still don't know how to negotiate for their needs. They give orders or make demands rather than dialogue with others. Being able to negotiate for our needs is an advanced skill that frequently isn't developed until the late Mature cycle. Before we can negotiate, we have to be aware of our needs, appreciate the needs of others, and be able to talk about our feelings, all lessons begun in the Baby cycle. In the Baby cycle, some progress is made in these areas, but not before the Baby soul's lack of skillfulness creates enough conflict to motivate him or her to behave differently. Needless to say, relationships are particularly challenging and painful for those at this stage of evolution.

Being able to love grows out of successful experiences with others. The Baby cycle is a time for increasing our ability to love. And although the challenges from relationships are the greatest, the strides made in learning to love also may be great. Usually, the soul provides Baby souls with ample opportunity to grow in love. Those in this cycle expend considerable energy in their relationships, particularly in their love relationships. This continues to be true for the Young cycle. You could say that these two cycles provide a crash course in relationships and, consequently, in love. But love at this stage is personal love, not unconditional love, which is present only sporadically until the late Old cycle. Sharing, negotiating, trusting, cooperating, accepting, nurturing, and letting go are all part of learning to love another person, which is one of the tasks of the Baby cycle.

In the beginning of the Baby cycle, we don't share, negotiate, trust, cooperate, accept, nurture, or let go of others. We learn these things by being in relationships that demand them. Relationships at this stage are like a game of tug-of-war, with each person fighting to get his or her needs met. In the Baby cycle, we don't understand that if we meet someone's needs, he or she is likely to want to meet ours. By the end of the Young cycle we know this, but it takes struggling with relationships for many, many lifetimes before we give up our needs long enough to see that we benefit from giving to others.

For Baby souls, the most difficult aspect of learning to share and cooperate is learning to trust. The Baby soul's us-versus-you mentality makes trusting others particularly difficult. Trust requires letting down our guard and accepting someone as an ally, which doesn't come easily to Baby souls. Once Baby souls have accepted someone, betrayal is a serious offense because they see betrayal as a direct threat to their survival. When betrayal does occur, it's hard for Baby souls to trust again. But since a relationship is almost impossible without trust, Baby souls are forced to open themselves up again or be lonely.

Trust is partly responsible for the push-pull that goes on in the Baby soul's relationships. "I don't trust you, but I need you" leads to possessiveness and jealousy. So along with control and non-acceptance, possessiveness and jealousy are other themes in the lives of Baby souls. These feelings aren't usually overcome until well into the Mature cycle, when we become much more understanding of the needs of others.

Baby souls' relationships become tangled by their jealousy, possessiveness, and need to control others. But even though these feelings create a great deal of pain for them, Baby souls don't easily let go of their relationships. In many cases, leaving a relationship isn't the answer anyway because Baby souls will just recreate other painful relationships until they change their attitudes and behavior.

Emotional growth takes lifetimes. Learning to trust, accept, share, cooperate, and let go are important lessons on the road to unconditional love, and they can't be rushed. Unconditional love is love without conditions. To love unconditionally, we have to be willing to get nothing from love except the joy of loving. But Baby souls are in relationships to be loved, accepted, appreciated, and cared for, and they have difficulty reciprocating. As they try to get love from others, they eventually learn to give it because that's the only way they will get what they want. By the end of our journey, we learn to give to others without any thought of reward.

Baby souls' intellectual interests are narrow. They take little interest in issues that fall outside their immediate concerns. Their intellectual world revolves around communicating and defending their viewpoints, which are usually unsubstantiated by research, study, or objective analysis. Baby souls aren't yet capable of objectivity or understanding the world from other points of view. At this stage, their feelings and intellect don't function separately enough to give them enough objectivity to analyze the ideas they encounter. Ideas that don't fit their perceptions are discounted and left unexamined. There will come a time in the Young cycle when this will no longer be true, but for now, narrow intellectual interests and a lack of intellectual investigation are typical.

Baby souls are determined to maintain their position at all costs. Children who don't follow parental opinion are excluded from the family, wives are beaten, feuds are fought, and laws are broken, all in the name of upholding the Baby soul's honor. Honor to Baby souls means maintaining their position of power and dominance. To them, power ensures their survival, and they get power through control. Their need for power and control stems from the amount of fear they feel.

Baby souls aren't convinced they can navigate the world safely without striking before they are struck or fighting before they are challenged. They are the ones for whom might is right, and what is right is what they say is right. If you argue with them, they will fight. They see even minor disagreements as potentially threatening to their survival. This may not be rational, but they aren't particularly rational or informed. They act on their feelings, which are often fear and anger.

Once their anger and fear have been dissipated, Baby souls might have some remorse, but it won't be over the damage they've done or what they fought about but over the consequences they're likely to be facing. It's particularly important for those at this stage to meet the consequences of their actions so that they begin to learn to manage their behavior and appreciate its effect on others. Guilt is just developing at this stage, and negative consequences develop it. Later on, guilt will come from true compassion for the victim, but not until negative consequences are felt first.

One of the important emotional lessons of the Baby cycle is learning to control anger and fear so that it doesn't harm others. The amount of fear in this cycle shouldn't be underestimated. There is more fear in this cycle than in any other except the Infant cycle. Baby souls feel threatened even by circumstances others don't find threatening, but Baby souls mask much of their fear in aggressive behavior, not wanting to give others an advantage over them. If the degree of their anger and aggression is any measure of their fear, we can conclude that their fear is great.

Aggressive impulses are more of a problem in the Baby cycle than in any other. Although aggressive impulses remain strong in the Young cycle, they're likely to be channeled into constructive activities, at least by the end of that cycle. But in the Baby cycle, we aren't yet able to sublimate and transform our aggressive impulses. Controlling them is the best that can be expected at this stage, and many Baby souls are unable to do that. Some control over our impulses is usually only achieved after we've already harmed someone and suffered the consequences.

Incarceration has been useful throughout history to help younger souls control their impulses by preventing them from acting on their feelings and by punishing their previous lapses in control. Incarceration is necessary and helpful in these instances. But we should be careful not to conclude that those at other stages of evolution or those who've committed nonviolent crimes benefit from these same conditions. Since few are rehabilitated in the prison system, only those for whom rehabilitation would be a waste of time should be placed there. In many cases, these are Baby souls. Some Young souls still need the restrictive punishment that incarceration delivers, but most souls beyond the Baby cycle would benefit more from educational and psychological approaches. As for Infant souls, they usually don't turn to violence except as a last resort. Incarceration might be necessary for them, but if the environment is abusive, incarceration is likely to do more harm than good. Infant souls are already so vulnerable and fearful that punishment only increases their fear and desire to escape reality. Our prison system needs to take into account what each person needs to be rehabilitated. Some need incarceration, while others need education, psychotherapy, or nurturing.

CHAPTER 3
Youth

THE YOUNG CYCLE

Most of the people on earth are Young souls. The United States is a Young soul country, as is this planet. What this means is that most of the people in this country and on this planet are Young souls. In fact, there are more Young souls in the United States than in any other country. When you understand what the Young soul cycle is about, this should come as no surprise. People reincarnate in situations in which they can best learn their lessons. When the lessons pertain to material acquisition and attainment of power and prestige, as they do in the Young cycle, the environment has to provide the potential for these. Because the United States is the most prosperous country with the most freedom to explore one's potentials, it's the training ground for many Young souls. This chapter refers to the people of the United States as exemplifying Young soul tendencies, but please remember that Young souls inhabit every part of the world and also that many in the United States are not Young souls.

In this cycle, the ego is very much in control, and Young souls have little access to their true nature in their everyday lives, although everyone, regardless of their soul age, experiences their true nature at times. These experiences are rare in the earlier cycles but more frequent as we evolve. Young souls are apt to distrust these experiences because such experiences are foreign to them, while older souls actively seek them out. This partly explains why speaking to Young souls about transcendent experiences or the quest for them is difficult. They are immersed in a quest of a different sort—a quest for power, prestige, wealth, beauty, and acclaim. It's not surprising, then, that Los Angeles and New York City are heavily populated with Young souls.

The outstanding characteristic of Young souls is their self-centeredness. Their egocentricity is more willful and intentioned than in earlier cycles. While Infant and Baby souls are incapable of moving beyond egocentricity, Young souls can, but they choose to indulge their desire for attention and power even at the expense of others. This is a time for exploration and self-development, not for appreciating the needs of others. By the end of the Young cycle, this will change, but not before the Young soul's needs and desires are fully explored.

The Young cycle is the "me cycle." Young souls, like teenagers, are learning who they are. They do this by trying on various roles. This helps them discover their talents and decide where to put their energy in future lifetimes. Although some Young souls are avidly pursuing athletics or honing other physical skills, this cycle is mostly for exploring various potentials rather than developing any one specialty. It's a time for exploring many occupations and lifestyles as a way of determining the direction of our future lifetimes. By the end of the Young cycle, we will have a sense of what talents and goals we want to pursue in our remaining lifetimes.

Young souls are interested in activities that bring recognition, material comforts, and prestige. As a result, Young souls aren't likely to be found in service professions or monasteries, for example. Attaining the desires of the ego—fame, recognition, comfort, beauty, security, wealth, and power—and discovering what it means to have them are major lessons of this cycle. The desires of the ego will be achieved, fulfilled, and in most cases glutted in this cycle before their impermanence and emptiness is realized. Some of this striving for power and prestige continues into the Mature cycle and, for some, even into the Old cycle. If it serves a purpose to encounter these lessons again, even an Old soul might make pre-life choices that will bring up these issues. The desire for prestige, power, and comfort may still be great in later lifetimes, especially given an astrology chart and environment that feed the desire for these things.

Given this, it isn't surprising to find Young souls in the entertainment industry, business, sports, or other areas where they can attain wealth and prestige. Their desire for these things motivates them to develop skills. Once some skills are acquired and the lessons of the Young cycle are completed, they will be ready to serve in a way that was not possible before this cycle. But for now, self-discovery is a necessary stage of development. Just as we can't expect teenagers to make great contributions to the world, we can't expect Young souls to either. There's a time for everything.

Another area of learning in this cycle is relationships. The lessons of the Baby cycle persist as Young souls continue to struggle with issues of trust, jealousy, possessiveness, sharing, and cooperation. At least Young souls have learned that sharing and cooperation are necessary to maintain a relationship, although they don't always do these things. When they do, they often expect to get something in exchange.

The style of loving of Young souls is still miles away from the ideal of unconditional love, but one step closer than in the Baby cycle. Young souls still expect others to meet their needs even if Young souls don't reciprocate. Furthermore, Young souls judge a relationship on how well it does this without accepting a similar responsibility. In this way, they are still like children, expecting to be provided for without giving in return. Usually their rationale for this is that their presence in the relationship should be enough for their partner.

Young souls are most often found in love relationships with other Young souls or Baby souls. They prefer to be with others who are like them. This isn't because they have difficulty getting along with others, like Baby souls, but because other Young souls will work with them to achieve their goals and not question their values.

Mature souls and Young souls aren't particularly compatible unless the Mature soul caters to the Young one, which does happen sometimes. Because Mature souls are conscious of the needs of others and often anxious to provide for them, a symbiotic relationship may be established between a Young soul and a Mature one. Although these relationships may not be particularly healthy, they may serve some other purpose.

Old souls are not particularly compatible with Young souls either because their goals are opposing: Young souls are indulging the cravings of the ego, while Old souls are trying to transcend them. Old souls present Young ones with a perspective they aren't ready for. This perspective doesn't offend Young souls as much as confuse them, since they have no basis for understanding it. On the other hand, Old souls are challenged by Young souls to be tolerant, which is something they need to learn. Old souls need to accept that what they've already learned can only be learned by Young souls through their own evolution.

Family relationships hold less importance for Young souls than for Baby souls. The Young cycle lacks the family loyalty and family involvement of the Baby cycle. Nevertheless, family relationships provide important lessons for Young souls about values. Until their values are readjusted, their families suffer from the Young soul's self-centeredness and preoccupation with self enhancement.

The families of Young souls are often neglected and treated as if their purpose is to serve the Young soul. By the Mature cycle, this attitude has to change. One way this is accomplished is through a family crisis, which demonstrates the importance of family and motivates Young souls to turn inward for a change. Although they aren't likely to stay with counseling once the crisis has subsided, family crises force Young souls to examine themselves. This self-examination reaches a peak in the Mature cycle, when it becomes nearly an obsession, but a productive one.

What's happening now in many American families exemplifies Young soul lessons. In the Young cycle, individualism and competitiveness replace the tribal mentality of the earlier cycles. Other people are seen by Young souls as a threat to success and security rather than a source of support. Young souls see the world through competitive eyes, as something to be conquered and used. It's not surprising, then, that so many in our culture go off to work intent on establishing their superiority in the world. This places a premium on work and time, so people need to work harder and longer to stay on top, which often leaves their emotional needs unmet.

Young souls naturally try to meet their emotional needs as efficiently as possible, since efficiency improves their chances of being on top. Marriage is a way to do that. But because Young souls usually have other Young souls as partners, who also want to achieve, this lifestyle can be unsatisfying. The solution is not to have both people vying in the market place, as is happening today, but for each to be involved in both family and career.

Young souls need both family and achievement. An important task of this cycle is integrating these two aspects of life so that each influences the other. Then, familial values will be brought into the marketplace and the quest for identity, tempering behavior so that the ego doesn't operate unchecked.

One characteristic of American culture that reflects Young soul consciousness is the need for constant activity and fun. The pastimes of Young souls stimulate the senses: eating, drinking, watching movies and television, listening to music, dancing, sex, games, and sports. Young souls are focused on physical pleasures. They never seem to tire of feeding the endless hungers of the ego.

It's not that the desire for sensual pleasures diminishes as we evolve, but the importance of them does. While Young souls organize their lives around meeting these cravings, older souls find satisfaction in intellectual exploration, intimate relationships, meditation, nature, and developing their talents.

From the standpoint of the Mature and Old cycles, Young souls are superficial and frivolous. Young souls, like Americans in general, don't value something unless it helps them attain wealth, sex, beauty, comfort, material security, or power. American television programs and movies reflect Young souls' interest in these things. Attaining them is a Young soul's raison d'être, but this life purpose is unique to Young souls. Mature and Old souls have very different goals and values, not yet reflected in American society as a whole.

The United States was founded on ideals that were the values and goals of older souls. It's interesting to see what Young souls have done with the freedoms they've inherited from these more advanced souls. Among other things, freedom in America has come to mean free enterprise, which frequently puts material values over ethical and spiritual ones. This undoubtedly will change as the soul level in the United States evolves.

Young souls have maintained the freedoms they inherited from those who were ahead of their time, mainly because it was advantageous. If Baby or Infant souls had inherited such freedoms, the United States would probably be very different. Our freedoms probably would have eroded into dictatorship or monarchy. But this doesn't mean that countries that have monarchies or dictatorships are necessarily Infant or Baby soul countries. There are many Mature and Old souls in every oppressed nation. Baby souls and some Young souls will seize opportunities for power anywhere those opportunities arise.

Like Americans, Young souls have a "live for today"

philosophy, which reflects their lack of depth and spiritual investigation. There's little spiritual questioning in this cycle. Most Young souls either follow their parents' religion or drop it altogether in deference to their worldly goals. They see religion as something that happens on Sunday and are content to leave that aspect of life to ministers and others. If Young souls are challenged to think more deeply about spirituality, they're likely to settle into a well traveled path. Not until the Mature cycle does deeper questioning occur. Even then, the religious beliefs of Mature souls are still likely to be more traditional than those of Old souls, who seek their own path and become their own ministers.

America's eating habits also reflect the preferences of Young souls, who are content to eat food that tastes good. Unless they are threatened with illness, Young souls aren't likely to eat healthfully. The proliferation of fast food restaurants is a testament to Young souls' preoccupation with taste and time. Their eating habits are heavily influenced by advertising, which glamorizes certain foods. Although Young souls are more objective than Infant or Baby souls, they're still easily impressed by promises for greater sex appeal, more fun, and better taste. The advertising industry in the United States clearly caters to the Young soul populace.

Another phenomenon in the United States that reflects the tastes of Young souls is the interest in sports, video games, and other competitive forms of entertainment. Competition is entertainment to Young souls. They enjoy competing and watching others compete. It's not surprising, then, that the United States takes athletic competition so seriously and considers its expertise in this area representative of its worldly power. The Olympic games are nonviolent displays of power that prove to the world the strength of the competing nations. The world of Mature and Old souls would have less emphasis on competition and more on competency in other areas.

The Young soul cycle is a time when those who want to become athletes hone these skills to perfection. The drive for beauty, physical perfection, glory, and excellence of the Young cycle is frequently channeled into developing and refining athletic skills. Although not all athletes are Young souls, many get their start and even achieve fame in this cycle. The athletic events most appealing to them are ones that display brute strength and aggressive competitiveness. Other sports requiring sensitivity and expression, such as dancing and skating, are more likely to be the choice of Mature and Old souls.

The United States is also known for its tolerance. Likewise, Young souls allow other people their differences as long as those differences don't interfere with attaining the Young soul's goals. Young souls are especially likely to disregard differences among people if it's to the Young soul's benefit. But Young souls aren't opposed to taking advantage of those who are different either. One example of this is the abuse of migrant workers. As a rule, Young souls don't fight for the rights of the oppressed unless it will elevate their own status or advance their own goals.

Young souls are pragmatic; their ethics bend according to their needs and desires. Although by this time they have a moral code, Young souls don't always apply it if it's not to their advantage. This is the most hypocritical cycle of all. The sensitivity of Mature souls prohibits them from similar hypocrisy, but this is also due to their greater objectivity and rationality. Young souls still suffer from subjectivity, especially when it comes to their own interests. Their thinking on this doesn't clear until somewhere in the Mature cycle.

Young souls find it hard to see themselves objectively, although objectivity is greater than in the Infant and Baby cycles. Their desires cloud their ability to see themselves except as they would like to be seen. So when confronted about their shortcomings, Young souls not only make up elaborate explanations, but also believe them. Young souls need to learn to be honest and admit their failings before they'll be able to grow beyond this cycle into a new relationship with themselves and others. Perhaps some comparisons could be drawn with the United States on this point too.

CHAPTER 4
Maturity

THE MATURE CYCLE

The Mature cycle is very different from the earlier ones. By this time in someone's evolution, most of the basic lessons have been mastered, particularly those pertaining to survival and managing emotions. New lessons and challenges present themselves in this cycle, as we gaze at the world through eyes that appreciate the feelings and perceptions of others. But although we accept the diversity of people and viewpoints at this stage in our development, this diversity often confuses us. We don't have the understanding yet to put it all in perspective. Establishing a philosophy for understanding and coping with this diversity is one of the main tasks of this cycle.

The ability to accept and understand the differences between people is one of the outstanding characteristics separating Mature souls from younger ones. While Young souls tolerate those who don't get in their way, Mature souls tolerate even those who do. They are intrigued by the differences in people. Trying to understand these differences becomes a motivating force in this cycle.

In the process, Mature souls question themselves and their own motives. This marks a tremendous shift. In the Mature cycle, for the first time, we are able to be objective and honest about our perceptions of ourselves, but the unrelenting self-analysis of this cycle creates considerable anxiety and psychic discomfort. By the Old cycle, we will have learned to balance this self-analysis with gentleness and compassion for ourselves. But for now, this stage of self-questioning and self-doubt is a necessary one.

Another major shift is that Mature souls have a greater capacity for loving unconditionally than younger souls. Unconditional love is a rare phenomenon for souls in the earlier cycles, although it sometimes occurs between family members. In the Mature cycle, for the first time, we experience unconditional love for those outside our immediate family.

Another distinguishing characteristic of the Mature cycle is the emergence of the desire to serve. Before this, we're primarily involved in self-development, a prerequisite to service. The shift from self-service to service happens, in part, because Mature souls are finally able to put themselves in someone else's shoes. Unfortunately, they don't just empathize with other people's pain, they often feel responsible for it, unnecessarily!

Guilt is one of the more common emotions of this cycle. Although guilt serves us well in this cycle, providing the driving force behind many of our accomplishments, eventually it has to be discarded. Unlike Young souls who are driven by greed, comfort, security, and the desire for power, Mature souls are driven by guilt, anxiety, confusion, alienation, and longing. They are all too aware of their failings and vulnerability. They seek peace and protection from the onslaught of life, not found in power, wealth, or prestige.

The Mature cycle marks the beginning of the search for understanding, spurred on by the angst created by the Mature soul's newfound sensitivity. Although in this cycle we have more understanding than in earlier cycles, our new awareness of others undermines our earlier certainty about ourselves, which has yet to be replaced by another way of seeing life. So Mature souls are lost in a sea of ideas and varying perceptions, wondering which of the many ways of viewing life will provide the answers they seek. They move from one philosophy and theory to the next in search of answers.

It shouldn't be surprising, then, that for most this is the cycle in which the greatest intellectual development takes place. Mature souls exercise their intellect by reading and choosing life purposes that often demand high levels of intellectual expertise. Mature souls often engage in specialized studies because advanced education is usually necessary to make the contributions to society that Mature souls so long to make. Intellectual exploration soothes their restless seeking and fulfills their desire to live a meaningful life.

The intellect of Mature souls is also enhanced by increased objectivity in this cycle, which enables them to use their minds unencumbered by their emotions. The freeing up of the mind from the emotions allows the intellect to advance by leaps and bounds, in part because interests are no longer circumscribed by opinions and feelings.

Another difference between the Mature cycle and earlier ones is an increasing interest in psychology. Before the Mature cycle, we don't try to understand our behavior or that of others. Our responses are automatic and conditioned by those around us. In the Mature cycle this changes, when the drive for psychological understanding becomes compelling.

In the Mature cycle, exploring feelings, motivations, and needs becomes paramount. This inner exploration is a necessary stage, preparing us for a different relationship to our feelings later in the Old cycle. Once we learn to be aware of, acknowledge, and accept our feelings, as we do in the Mature cycle, we can step aside from them in the Old cycle. Detachment from the emotions, characteristic of the Old cycle, can't occur until the groundwork for it is laid in the Mature cycle.

Guilt, shame, depression, anxiety, apathy, and despair are the characteristic emotions of the Mature cycle. Anger is less common in this cycle than in any other cycle except the Old. And when anger is expressed or even felt, it's usually accompanied by guilt. Anger is more likely to be repressed in this cycle than in the earlier ones, but that doesn't prevent anger from wrecking havoc with our well-being and health.

Repressed anger is at the root of the anxiety of this cycle. It's also often the cause of psychosomatic illnesses and other physical complaints. In this cycle, repression is discovered as a new way to cope with anger and the fear and guilt involved in expressing anger. But by the end of this cycle, we've usually developed some acceptance of and detachment from our anger so that these feelings don't need to be repressed or turned in on ourselves (retroflected) in the form of self-blame, self-mutilation, or physical complaints, all characteristic of this cycle.

Mature souls eventually go beyond repression, retroflection, and controlling their anger to talking about it skillfully. They even begin to learn how not to create anger and how to be in relationship to it when it does arise.

Many of the fears of the earlier cycles have subsided by the Mature cycle as a result of increased inner resources and abilities, but other fears arise to take their place. Fear of inadequacy and failure, fear of being alone, and fear of dying without having lived a meaningful life replace the fear of survival. These demons can't be grappled with on the outside. They have to be faced in an inner battle, for which many Mature souls enlist the help of professionals.

Psychotherapy suits Mature souls more than any other soul age because their psychological pain and interest in analysis are an impetus for change and self-discovery. Mature souls also are the ones most likely to become psychotherapists. Many of today's psychological theories and therapies were created by Mature souls. Nevertheless, many Old souls also become psychotherapists, since many of them have life purposes related to healing.

Depression and the despair, apathy, alienation, and boredom that accompany it are the most problematic feelings of this cycle. Unlike guilt and shame, which serve some purpose in motivating Mature souls to improve themselves, depression depletes their resources and inhibit their growth. Depression is immobilizing, making it difficult to get on with life. Nevertheless, depression serves as a warning sign, pointing to our belief in negativity and to life choices that may be out of alignment with our soul's plan. If someone gets emotional help or makes necessary changes because of depression, then the depression isn't a waste.

Mature souls often spend from one to several lifetimes

battling the depression of this cycle before they develop the inner strength and understanding needed to cope with negative feelings successfully. Learning to not be at the mercy of such feelings is an important step in our growth, which eventually leads to a more healthy relationship to feelings in the Old cycle, although negativity can remain an issue for much of the Old cycle.

Despite the Mature soul's greater capacity to love, learning to love takes an unusual turn in the Mature cycle. Mature souls have more difficulty loving themselves than they do loving others. Before this cycle, we have difficulty loving anyone who isn't like us, but Mature souls have difficulty loving anyone who is. In psychological terms, this phenomenon is called *projection*. It means that we see our failings in others and respond negatively to those individuals as a result.

The lesson with projection is to pay attention to what we dislike in others because that tells us what we need to reform in ourselves. Mature souls use this understanding to gain self-awareness. In this cycle, they are challenged to recognize their projections and re-own them so that those projections don't interfere with their ability to love themselves or others. This is no small task, and it takes the entire Mature cycle as well as the Old cycle to accomplish it.

In the Mature cycle, our behavior and emotions are less likely to interfere with forming satisfying relationships than in the earlier cycles. The Mature soul's inclination to accept blame, feel guilt, and try to understand others are all advantages in building relationships. Moreover, because the intellect is less colored by emotions than earlier, Mature souls can communicate more clearly with others than younger souls. These qualities make negotiation possible. In the Mature cycle, we develop our negotiation skills and put them to good use in our relationships.

The most difficult relationships for Mature souls are their love relationships. Mature souls still feel some jealousy and possessiveness, and they still haven't mastered intimacy. But these issues don't prevent them from establishing meaningful relationships. Mature souls do develop meaningful, long-lasting relationships, which enhance their understanding of themselves and people in general. Their deep desire for intimacy motivates them to work hard at maintaining these sometimes challenging relationships, which provide the training ground for much of the emotional growth that takes place in this cycle.

The emotional growth of this cycle establishes a foundation for the spiritual growth of the Old cycle. As we develop greater understanding of others and ourselves in the Mature cycle, our ability to put our emotions and the events of our lives in perspective increases. Through the emotional work accomplished in this cycle, we become better able to experience ourselves apart from our personalities, our bodies, our minds, and our emotions. This learning continues into the Old cycle and becomes the focus of the later lifetimes of the Old cycle.

THE OLD CYCLE

Individuals in each cycle have some of the tendencies of the earlier ones. This is as true for Old souls as anyone else. Although each cycle has its own perceptions and unique way of operating, underlying this, we human beings are more alike than we are different. It's a mistake to think Old souls don't have the same problems that younger ones do. Nevertheless, even though Old souls struggle with the same problems, their perceptions of them, the resources they have to bring to them, and their approaches to them are different.

The outstanding characteristic of Old souls is their ability to "live and let live." This attitude, which began developing in the Young cycle, becomes fully integrated in the Old cycle. Mature souls follow this motto as best they can, but they have difficulty letting *themselves* "live." Mature souls believe that, although differences are fine, it's still better to be one way than another. Old souls, on the other hand, feel that differences are not only fine, but also purposeful, with everyone having a unique path.

Old souls don't feel the confusion about their life purpose that younger souls do. The reason for this is that the intuition functions better in the Old cycle than in earlier ones. This is the first cycle in which we can be consistently guided by our intuition. Before that, our intuition is sporadic and either inhibited or distorted by the intellect or emotions. By the Old cycle, the intellect has become a force unto itself, the emotions are less compelling, and our true nature is more accessible. These factors distinguish Old souls from younger ones.

The Old soul's ability to have emotions without being ruled by them is an important evolutionary step. This is the endpoint in the evolution of the emotions, since we can't get rid of emotions altogether and wouldn't want to.

Old souls also know how to use their egos without being ruled by them. Old souls observe the ego's antics without being taken in by it. They relate to the ego as a good parent relates to a child, with compassion but without indulging its childish desires and reactions. Moreover, Old souls are able to make choices from this place of objectivity, which is actually another state of consciousness. It is, in fact, our natural state.

Each cycle has its own state of consciousness, which is another way of saying that each cycle has its own perceptions. The Old cycle's state of consciousness includes frequent experiences of our true nature, of our divine Self. Just as someone who hasn't experienced a certain cycle can't really understand those who have, someone who hasn't experienced a certain state of consciousness can't really understand it and may even question its existence. This results in misunderstandings, which can't be remedied until each of us has advanced through every stage. Since this will never happen, we are destined to be challenged by these differences.

Old souls aren't particularly concerned about differences in opinion. They're less likely to want to please others than Mature souls, less likely to manipulate others than Young souls, and less likely to try to change others than Baby souls. They know what's right for themselves. They pursue this with consideration for others, but also regardless of them. As a result, they often have conflicts with their families, and many are considered black sheep. This doesn't particularly disturb Old souls, since they consider themselves part of a greater family of humankind, one not bound by ties of blood, nationality, or race.

As a result of their many lifetimes, Old souls don't see the differences between people as much as the similarities. Our experiences are stored within us, so by the Old cycle we have been many different characters, and on some level we remember how each of these characters felt. The compassion we've gained from these experiences shapes our perceptions of others and, consequently, our behavior toward them. Because Old souls see themselves in others, treating others as they would like to be treated comes naturally.

Past-life experiences also develop our wisdom and understanding. On a deep level, Old souls recall their lessons from former lifetimes and draw on the wisdom they gained from those lifetimes in making choices. As a result, the challenges Old souls face are more often to further their growth than a consequence of unwise choices, as with younger souls.

This cycle, like all others, has its lessons. But for Old souls, contributing to life is as important to their growth as their lessons are. The life purposes of this cycle and the Mature cycle pertain more to using our talents in service than they do to learning lessons, which is the focus in earlier cycles. By the Old cycle, the basic lessons of life have been mastered, and service is paramount.

Many of the lessons remaining in the Old cycle pertain to service. Two of these lessons are learning to serve unselfishly and learning to serve appropriately. The first, learning to serve unselfishly, is an ideal that is never entirely realized except in the last one or two lifetimes. Until then, there are different stages or levels of service. The first is serving with the intent of benefiting from it. The second is serving for the joy of it and its benefits. This is only slightly different from the third level of service, which is detached from the outcome.

While learning to serve, we discover that there's a right and a wrong way to serve. Right service doesn't do things for others that they'd be better off doing for themselves but helps people become more self-sufficient. If we do things for others that they can and should do for themselves, we rob them of the joy of achieving on their own and the growth accomplished by their efforts. In doing this, we may actually inhibit their growth instead of help them.

Learning to give in a way that helps others grow is the first lesson of right service. The second is learning to serve in a way that doesn't stunt our own growth. For this, we need to distinguish between service and self-sacrifice. This distinction is learned slowly and, in many cases, painfully by being left feeling empty and used. Right service is enriching to both the server and the served and leaves neither feeling helpless nor depleted.

Psychic development is another major area of learning in the Old cycle. Psychic development usually begins in this cycle, but it's a slow and gradual process that proceeds uniquely for each person. So it's difficult to make generalizations about psychic development. Although the potential for psychic development exists in this cycle, whether that potential is developed, what form it takes, and to what extent it is developed is a matter of choice. Some experience some initial psychic development and then choose to discontinue it. When that's the case, the soul will deliver the lessons related to psychic development some other way. But it's rare that someone doesn't partake in some psychic development in the Old cycle and, consequently, its lessons.

The first and most difficult lesson related to psychic development is ego detachment. Learning this is never easy because the ego enjoys getting attention and admiration for any special abilities, and psychic abilities are no exception. As a result, those just developing or regaining psychic abilities from former lifetimes commonly draw attention to themselves. Some are rebuked for their arrogance early on and learn this lesson before they have far to fall. But some win the hearts and confidence of others enough to gain some recognition and status, only to fall later and harder. In either case, a fall is likely. This will reorient the individual to using his or her skills more humbly. This pattern is common. Those who don't have a problem with humility have probably fallen in a previous lifetime and are just not making this mistake again.

The proper use of psychic skills is in service to others, but until we've passed through the various stages of service, the ideal of serving with detachment is just that—an ideal. Until that ideal is approached, we're likely to be tempted to serve the ego rather than others with our psychic abililties. Here, the issue may not only be pride, but also a drive for power. Any use of psychic skills to gain an inordinate amount of money or influence is bound to backfire, as will using those abilities to bolster one's pride. It's not that there's anything sacred about psychic abilities or that someone shouldn't be paid for them, but the soul will use psychic development to teach us ego detachment and right service when the opportunity arises.

Discernment is another lesson related to psychic development. Old souls are learning to differentiate between psychic impressions and their own thoughts or feelings. Because this takes practice, early in our psychic development we're likely to make mistakes. This is only a problem if we assume we're always correct and we give that impression to others. Many today are at this stage, dispensing inconsistent and inaccurate information without even realizing it. Eventually, they'll discover they are doing this, and the lesson will be learned. Until then, a lot of damage can be done to others and to the reputation of psychics and more reputable healers.

The final lesson of psychic development concerns another kind of abuse of power: giving our power away to others. The risk of doing this is particularly great with channeling, where information is received from a disembodied source. Many who are disembodied are qualified to give information, but many are not. Even those who are qualified aren't infallible. Everyone who uses channeled information should understand this. Handling this information wisely is their responsibility. If they don't, they have no one else to blame and no one else to suffer the consequences. Allowing spirits to make our decisions for us, or allowing anyone else to do so for that matter, is an abdication of our will. When we do that, we relinquish our freedom to make choices, which is our sacred right and responsibility.

Another task of the Old cycle is eliminating old patterns that inhibit our growth. We all have had experiences in former lifetimes that have negatively shaped our behavior. Some of these patterns have the potential for interfering with our growth or life purpose. Healing them is important work in the Old cycle.

This healing is usually accomplished by the soul by selecting a time to be born that will reflect the energies needed to overcome these blocks. Our astrology chart is a picture of the energies in the universe at the time of our birth, which are reflected in us and create certain tendencies. If we need to eliminate a certain pattern from the past, we will choose to be born under energies that make these tendencies difficult to continue.

Another task of the Old cycle is to increase our compassion and understanding. In this cycle, compassion is developed differently than in other cycles. Most Old souls don't need to experience deprivation to learn compassion, as is often the case in earlier cycles. The compassion of Old souls is enhanced through serving those who are suffering.

Developing a philosophy that defines the meaning of life is another important task of the Old cycle. Most Old souls are eager to understand why life is the way it is, who we are, and why we are here. Old souls are usually drawn to less traditional philosophies, although they might combine the similarities of traditional religions into their own understanding. Buddhism is particularly attractive to Old souls because it embraces all humanity and all faiths. Old souls work to bring the various religions under one roof, proclaiming their similarities rather than their differences. They also are the ones working toward brotherhood, equality, and freedom for all.

Democracy is a very progressive notion. It acknowledges that everyone has the potential to benefit society and the right and responsibility to do so in his or her own way. This concept originated in the minds of certain Old souls, and it characterizes this cycle. Since Old souls see themselves in others, it is only natural for them to create a political system that recognizes everyone as equally valuable, although not necessarily equal.

Obviously, not everyone is equal in inner resources, talents, intelligence, wisdom, and understanding. But democracy and Old souls recognize the intrinsic value of human life and the value of diversity, and that is what they celebrate. Old souls embrace diversity. They genuinely feel that not only is it okay for you to be you and for me to be me, but it's all the better that we are different.

OTHER FACTORS THAT INFLUENCE BEHAVIOR

Our soul age is the primary factor explaining our behavior and perceptions, but there are other secondary factors. These secondary factors are the astrology chart and other esoteric influences, past-life experiences, and the environment. The influence of these secondary factors is limited and can't make up for the differences between people more than one cycle apart. For instance, a Baby soul is never likely to be mistaken for a Mature or Old soul, nor an Old soul for a Young one. Nevertheless, to fully understand human behavior, we need to keep these secondary factors in mind. Each of us is a complex and unique blend of many factors that influence how we perceive and respond to life.

Besides soul age, the most compelling factor is the astrology chart. Our chart represents the personality we've chosen for a particular lifetime. The chart is like a costume we put on for the time being. For that lifetime, we experience life through the energies of that chart, which reflect specific needs, drives, and ways of responding to life.

If our chart represents tendencies uncharacteristic of our soul age, we may seem different from our actual soul age. For example, an Old soul who has a chart with a Capricorn and Leo emphasis is likely to express a stronger desire for material acquisition and power than most Old souls and may not seem to be an Old soul because of these drives. Similarly, Young souls with an emphasis in the water signs are likely to show more sensitivity and compassion than is typical for their soul age.

Our past-life experiences also have an influence on our current perceptions and responses. For instance, a Young soul may choose to lead a sheltered, dependent life to heal from a trauma in a former lifetime. In that case, he or she may seem more like a fearful Infant or Baby soul than an independent, enterprising Young soul. Similarly, a Young soul who has had many lifetimes as a Pisces, for example, is likely to be more compassionate than others of his or her soul age.

The influences in our environment work the same way. For example, if an Old soul is raised in a fundamentalist Christian family, his or her spirituality is likely to have a stronger traditional component than other Old souls without that influence. Old souls who express their spirituality through traditional avenues have a broad-mindedness and love that transcends their denomination and includes everyone. The mark of an Old soul is this openness, not the form his or her spirituality takes.

Cultural influences also play a part in our responses and drives. For example, Old souls raised in the United States, a Young soul nation, are still likely to want the things valued by their culture—money, power, status, comfort, and beauty—although they're likely to feel conflicted about it. On the other hand, younger souls raised in India may appear older than they are because of that country's emphasis on spirituality.

The intent of this information is to promote acceptance, not apathy. It's easy to conclude from these descriptions that there's nothing we can do to change others. But that's not true. We're in this world to influence each other and share our perceptions. It's part of the plan for us to influence each other. We need each other this way. We're moved along through the various stages of evolution by the conflicts and challenges that result from our encounters with others. The interplay of people in the various cycles contributes to our evolution and our understanding of life's mysteries.

CHAPTER 5
Soul Age and Behavior

As we have seen, soul age affects our behavior and perceptions. In this chapter, we'll look more closely at certain behaviors and how they differ from one cycle to the next.

RAISING CHILDREN

Infant and Baby souls have many difficulties raising children. They don't have the resources yet to care for themselves, much less to care for someone else. So it's not unusual for Infant and Baby souls to be neglectful of their children, largely out of ignorance, but also because life is very stressful for Infant and Baby souls. They rarely intend to hurt their children and are often unaware they are causing harm. These parents need education as well as support from those who can help relieve their stress, model parenting, and give them a break from their children.

Infant and Baby souls raise their children as they were raised and rarely question their parents' beliefs or approaches. Likewise, they expect their children to follow in their footsteps and accept their beliefs without question. Although Infant and Baby soul children are likely to comply, older soul children often question the rigid rules and dogma of these parents, creating even more family stress and parental disappointment. As a result, family conflict stemming from rebellion is common in these homes. But this conflict is productive because it teaches these parents about individual differences, and in straining the limits of their coping abilities, it often brings these families to the attention of those who can help them.

Since these families can't handle their problems satisfactorily on their own, their success and the safety of their children often depend on getting help from those who can teach them effective parenting techniques and ways of coping with their stress. There will always be those who need special help, even into adulthood, who can't deal with the stresses of everyday life without ongoing support and education. We as a society need to accept responsibility for these youngest of souls. If we don't, who will? We owe them a hand up, just as we, presumably, were given help at that stage. In truth, we benefit as much as they do by helping them.

By the time we are Young souls, we're better able to handle the challenge of parenthood. Young souls can usually provide for their children materially, even if they still can't provide adequately for them emotionally. In these families, the children teach Young soul parents how to love by demanding that their parents give to them and become sensitive to their needs. Young soul parents eventually learn to love, to be more empathetic, and to give to their children. And through the love they come to have for their children, Young soul parents eventually learn to love others.

For Young soul parents, raising children is a constant challenge to their selfish desires. They constantly struggle with balancing their own needs with their children's. Young soul parents are similar to teenage parents who, not having had their own needs met, find it hard to give to their children willingly. Young soul parents do give to their children, but not until the Mature cycle is it done joyfully rather than out of obligation.

Young souls see their children as an obligation, which, like all their obligations, they take seriously. These parents have children because having children is what's done rather than because they understand and welcome the commitment. This is another way Young soul parents are like teenagers. Their capacity to love their children is also about as limited as it is for teenagers because Young soul parents have little ability to love unconditionally. Before the Mature cycle, children are loved because parents see them as belonging to them, as part of them. In the Mature cycle this changes, when children begin to be valued as individuals. This shift requires a degree of self-awareness and appreciation of individual differences that is absent until the Mature cycle.

Young soul parents are not unaware of their children's needs, as in earlier cycles, but they put their own needs before their children's. An example is a parent who insists that a child finish every bit of food on his or her plate because that's the parent's idea of what a good parent does. In this cycle, parental authority still takes precedence over the child's needs and feelings. It's not until the Mature and Old cycles that parents begin to listen to their children and negotiate with them. And yet, younger soul parents can learn to do this from older souls who model this for them.

In the Mature cycle, it's another story. Mature soul parents feel worried and guilty about their children. They are all too aware of the importance of their role as a parent. They feel that what their children become depends entirely on them, which is hardly true. Not until the Old cycle, do we realize that other factors are involved. Mature soul parents feel a responsibility to mold their children, not because they want them to be like themselves or because they're concerned about what others will think, as in earlier cycles, but because they're afraid that if their children don't turn out right, it will be their fault. If that happened, they would feel they hadn't done their duty or lived up to the standards they'd set for themselves.

Mature souls are forever seeking perfection, not living up to it, feeling guilty, and driving themselves to do better the next time. They project this desire for perfection onto their children, hoping their children will achieve what they, themselves, could not. So many Mature soul parents spend large sums of money on therapists, lessons, special educational opportunities, and other enriching experiences for their children. At least, if their children don't turn out, they can say they tried. And they do try, more than parents in any other cycle.

Mature soul parents bend over backwards to accommodate not only their children's physical and intellectual needs, but also their emotional needs. This leaves a child feeling cared about but perhaps a little too important. It can be scary for a child to feel so important. Not only that, the emphasis put on the child's feelings often leaves the child confused about what is expected of him or her. Sometimes children just need to be told what to do, but Mature soul parents often are afraid that this approach will harm their child's development. In truth, how children respond to the parenting they receive depends more on the child's soul age than on the approach. More than anything else, soul age needs to be considered in raising a child.

Old souls view their children with the respect with which they view all humanity. They are likely to feel that their children reflect the spirituality and closeness to God that the Old soul seeks. And this is often the role children do play for them. Old soul parents see parenting as a way of developing unconditional love and serving humanity on a more personal level. They accept the challenge of parenting as the grist for the mill that it is and for its many blessings. Because Old soul parents are equipped to handle challenging children, they are often given them and even request them before life. Parenting challenges provide the growth for which many Old souls yearn.

Old souls are also likely to use their intuition effectively in dealing with their children and to educate themselves about parenting. Unfortunately, all their wisdom, education, patience, and skill may not be enough when raising a very young soul. Fortunately, they are aware, at least on some level, that everyone is responsible for his or her own acts and that they can only do so much to help others. Because Old soul parents feel less identified with and responsible for their children than parents in earlier cycles, they're better able to accept the challenges of parenting.

Let's turn this around and look at what kind of parenting approaches children in each cycle need.

Infant and Baby souls need a supportive and nurturing environment. Anything that aggravates their fear will not help them grow. The best results with such children are obtained through gentleness and patience. Authoritarian and punitive approaches can actually be detrimental, causing Baby and Infant souls to either withdraw in fear or retaliate in destructive acts.

Love begets love in all cycles, but love is a must in the early ones. Old soul children may be able to withstand authoritarian and abusive parenting and become stronger as a result, but these approaches destroy Infant and Baby soul children. These children also don't benefit greatly from intellectual analysis because it is beyond them, although the sensitivity that's conveyed by trying to understand them is helpful to them.

Young soul children are not nearly as vulnerable as Infant and Baby soul children. Some ego strength has developed by this time. In fact, Young soul children need to have their limits clearly stated. If they don't have structure, they're likely to take advantage of authority figures and not learn to take responsibility for their actions. An authoritarian approach is more appropriate in the Young cycle than in any other cycle, although structure and discipline need to be tempered with love and consideration for the child's feelings.

Young soul children who sense that parents are taking advantage of their authority, a tendency common to Young and Baby soul parents, will either rebel or imitate their parents' abuse of power. So it's especially important that Young soul children have kindness and consideration modeled for them. Any approach used with Young soul children should also help them understand their feelings, since emotional growth is one of the tasks of this cycle.

Mature soul children are sensitive and usually don't need a heavy hand, although a lot depends on other factors such as the child's astrology chart. Abusive or authoritarian treatment on the part of the parents isn't as likely to cause violent or antisocial behavior in Mature soul children as depression, guilt, shame, and feelings of worthlessness, which can prevent the child from fulfilling his or her potential.

With Mature soul children, it's better to err on the side of leniency than strictness. This is because Mature soul children are more sensitive than younger souls and generally more intelligent and in control of their emotions. As a result, they're less likely to be difficult to raise, with shyness, depression, addictions, and other neurotic behaviors being more likely than antisocial or other disagreeable acts. Mature soul children want to please and, when given a chance, will go out of their way to perform well. Building their self-esteem should be the biggest concern. Parenting approaches that help these children understand their feelings and build confidence and self-acceptance work best.

Old soul children are full of questions about life, often deep ones. These questions need to be handled with respect. Making fun of these children's questions or giving simplistic answers will only undermine their confidence in themselves and in authority figures.

Old soul children and Old souls in general need to learn to trust themselves, to trust their heart. They usually know what is best for themselves and should be encouraged to follow their intuition. Old soul children need parents who trust them to make choices and who give them the information they need to make good choices. Because of their innate wisdom, Old soul children are likely to make good choices and learn from their mistakes. Consequently, these children can be given more freedom and responsibility than children in the other cycles.

Because of their inherent wisdom and adaptability, Old soul children tend to be easy to raise and able to survive any parenting approach. But that doesn't mean they thrive on being neglected. Although Old soul children can survive neglect and even become stronger as a result, they do best in an environment that acknowledges their individuality, intelligence, and needs. Even though they're likely to turn any experience to their advantage, respect and intelligent interchange will help them fulfill their potentials and prepare them to serve others as adults.

EDUCATION

The various soul ages have different views on education and different educational requirements. Infant souls need only the most basic education. Literacy isn't even necessary for them to grow as they need to. Their education best entails simple things like cooking, caring for themselves, and basic hygiene. Rarely do Infant souls even develop skills like pottery or basket weaving. Too much emphasis on education may frustrate Infant souls, cause them to rebel, make them feel inferior, or divert their energies away from other important tasks of this cycle. This is why few Infant souls reincarnate in technological societies, which require some degree of education. Their lives are simple and their education is best limited to the basics.

Baby souls are beginning to be able to master more complex assignments, and their education should be in keeping with that. But their education should continue to focus on practical skills rather than on intellectual analysis and abstract thinking. Significant intellectual advances during the Baby cycle can be achieved, but these advances are usually the result of hands-on experience with life, not academic exploration.

Because of their need for structure, Baby souls are likely to flourish in small towns and communities that clearly define the Baby soul's direction for him or her. Baby souls do best following in their parents' trade or staying involved in their community rather than stepping out on their own, where they're likely to feel lost and intellectually challenged.

Young souls show a marked change from other cycles in their views toward education and in their educational requirements. In American society and others where education means power and success, Young souls clamber for education, stretching themselves intellectually and growing by leaps and bounds intellectually in this cycle. However, Young souls are likely to dabble in this and that rather than develop expertise in any one area. Nevertheless, by the end of this cycle many are on their way to becoming experts in something.

This is the first cycle in which higher education is appropriate and beneficial. Young souls can benefit from the educational opportunities that complex societies offer, which is one reason they reincarnate in these societies. Unlike Infant and Baby souls, Young souls are capable of abstract manipulations, indicating an important shift in intellectual development.

Mature souls are specialists, requiring specialized education. They are the ones most likely to apply for post-graduate programs and other advanced studies. They, along with Old souls, are also the ones most likely to make intellectual discoveries capable of changing people's lives. Mature souls need access to a full range of educational opportunities. A Mature soul without these opportunities is lost and unlikely to fulfill his or her potentials.

The same could be said about Old souls, although they aren't attracted to educational environments that don't take into account the intuitive or humane side of life. Many Old souls have a disdain for academicians, whom they feel are shortsighted and out of touch with the true purpose of life.

Old souls often become teachers of life, and if credentials will help them, they're willing to get credentials. So unlike Mature souls, who pursue education for its own sake, Old souls seek it to achieve their goals or pass it by if their goals don't require it.

Old souls aren't concerned about what others might think of them if they don't have an education. Old souls have a sense of themselves as being valuable and capable without it. They are self-directed learners who know what they want to learn and can assemble the materials they need themselves. This makes Old souls particularly capable of leading others in intellectual explorations. As a result, they're the ones most likely to bring fresh ideas to society and to be in touch with future trends.

WORK

Infant souls are like Old souls in one respect: They frequently don't work at conventional jobs. But for Old souls this is a choice, while for Infant souls this happens more by default. Infant souls don't have the ability to sustain their concentration or efforts. It's not that they don't want to fit into society, but they can't. They work best when little is demanded of them intellectually and they aren't forced beyond their comfort range.

Infant souls fall apart when their basic needs aren't met and refuse to function beyond that point. Eventually, by necessity, they learn to stretch themselves. But forcing them doesn't help. What does help is kind encouragement and praise for staying with a task—and rewards. The more tangible and immediate the gratification, the more Infant souls are able to work for it. If a reward has no real value to them or if they have to wait too long for it, Infant souls aren't likely to do well. The problem is that Infant souls aren't internally motivated yet. Working for the pure satisfaction of it or for some other intrinsic reward doesn't come until well into the Baby cycle. Consequently, Infant souls need constant supervision and encouragement.

Baby souls aren't very different from Infant souls in their attitude toward work and the kind of work they enjoy, but Baby souls can stay with a job longer and handle more complex tasks, given adequate training and motivation. Baby souls are still largely motivated by external rewards and the desire to please others. This remains true until the end of the Baby cycle, when we begin to experience the satisfaction that comes from doing a good day's work.

In these early cycles, what the work is about isn't as important as the kind of work, which needs to be simple, practical, and usually physical. Not until later cycles does our work begin to reflect our personality, talents, and interests. Consequently, Baby souls often do jobs that others find unattractive. If a job pays their bills and they can do it, that's enough for them. Obviously, Baby souls are suited to many positions in industrialized society, although these positions are likely to become harder to come by as automation makes them unavailable. When this happens, Baby souls will probably reincarnate in simpler societies where they can work at crafts and other trades.

Young souls work in a variety of fields, still preferring physical tasks over intellectual ones. This begins to change by the second half of this cycle. Young souls aren't satisfied with the simple tasks of earlier cycles or with the lack of power and monetary reward that usually accompany simple tasks. Young souls are the shakers and movers of society, seeking high pressure jobs that will earn them the prestige and admiration they desire. These jobs also give Young souls an opportunity to learn about values, one of the tasks of this cycle.

Because the Young cycle is for sampling the smorgasbord of life, these lifetimes also may sample a smorgasbord of work experiences. It's not unusual for Young souls to hop from job to job looking for the one that will give them the glory they seek. The dream of wealth and riches drives us on in the Young cycle until the Mature cycle, when we're ready to settle into some kind of work that has deeper meaning to us. The Young cycle is also the first cycle in which we work for ourselves and manage others. By that time, the ego has developed enough to aspire to such positions and be able to handle them.

Mature souls look for work that is personally meaningful. Unlike in the earlier cycles, Mature souls measure the value of their work by the satisfaction it gives them and the value it has for society. Mature souls aren't opposed to working for others or within an organization as long as they have the freedom to operate according to their principles and preferences. They feel a responsibility to make this a better world. One way Mature souls try to do this is through the workplace.

Mature souls often succeed at affecting change in society because they have the interpersonal skills and intelligence to make their point and be taken seriously. So Mature souls are often found working within society's structures. Many are reformers, humanitarians, health professionals, and other service providers. Service professions appeal strongly to Mature souls, as does work that allows them to expand their intellectual potentials. Few Mature souls are blue-collar workers, but this changes in the Old cycle, when menial tasks may be taken on if these tasks don't interfere with the Old soul's goal of spiritual development.

In the Old cycle any kind of work is possible, although Old souls often don't choose conventional work. It's as if they know they've already done those things, so they don't feel a need to do them again. Still, they need to support themselves someway, so if an Old soul's life purpose doesn't involve intellectual accomplishment, he or she may just do simple tasks to get by.

Old souls are content with simple tasks because of their idealism and lack of concern with material assets. They won't sell themselves out for the luxuries of life, as Young souls are likely to do. This doesn't mean Old souls never attain riches. As many Old souls use their intelligence and talents to excel in the world as Young souls, but money is never their only motive.

Old souls who do make their mark through work usually feel a sense of mission, which is a hallmark of this cycle. So when their life purpose coincides with a specific kind of work, they'll be as driven to succeed as any Young soul. Old souls can be hard-hitting, but integrity and values guide their actions, not greed and ambition.

RECREATION

The various soul ages enjoy different forms of recreation and approach play differently. Infant souls aren't physically coordinated, and they aren't risk-takers. Consequently, many sports and outdoor activities don't appeal to Infant souls. They do enjoy simple games that improve their coordination, though, such as catch, as long as those games aren't competitive or threatening. On the rare occasions when Infant souls do play team sports, they need special consideration for their needs and feelings, like a young child or anyone with lesser capabilities would.

Because Infant souls have difficulty abandoning their fears and inhibitions, they don't let go to pleasure and fun very easily. They tend toward seriousness and solitude. Quiet, solitary activities appeal to them, such as relaxing in a hammock and gazing at the clouds, playing with clay or sand, making pictures, experimenting with simple musical instruments, stringing beads, whittling, or doing simple crafts.

Baby souls aren't very different from Infant souls in their recreational interests and capabilities, but they do have more ability and desire to participate with others in activities. Baby souls still aren't likely to enjoy highly competitive team sports, but they like noncompetitive versions of them. Mostly, they enjoy being alone and expressing themselves creatively in some form, such as drawing or music.

This changes dramatically in the Young cycle, when the emphasis is on competition and developing physical prowess. The Young cycle is a physical cycle, partly because physical prowess is one way of gaining power and control, which are important to Young souls. Underlying the Young soul's recreational choices is this drive for power. No longer being satisfied with relaxation or activities that don't enhance their standing in other people's eyes, Young souls use their free time to develop themselves in ways they feel others will value. So the recreational activities of Young souls challenge them physically, mentally, and socially and are a means for growth in this cycle. For delivering lessons, recreation is as important as other aspects of the Young soul's life.

Mature souls continue to use their recreational time in ways that they have in earlier cycles. For instance, if they enjoyed rowing in previous lifetimes, they will probably row in this cycle too, although their approach will be different.

Mature souls are less competitive with others but continue to be competitive with themselves. They're interested in improving their physical and mental agility but usually for reasons other than proving something to others or gaining acclaim. For example, a Mature soul may excel in swimming for the discipline it develops or in playing the piano for the joy it brings.

Because the Mature cycle is an introverted one, the creative arts are popular. Many Mature souls become proficient at the creative and expressive arts because they need to express their angst. So Mature souls find relief in the arts, reading, and sports, which allow them to channel and express their feelings in a socially acceptable way.

Old souls, like Infant souls, find more solitary ways to enjoy themselves. Few Old souls engage in highly competitive sports unless they've enjoyed that in the past. Many prefer to be alone to recoup their energy, either by reading, walking, listening to soothing music, or being with nature.

What Old souls enjoy doing depends mostly on what they've enjoyed in previous incarnations. This cycle continues to build on the creative talents and athletic interests of earlier cycles, but Old souls approach these things with less pressure and competition. Old souls look to these activities not only to recuperate from the stress of everyday life, but also to experience the transcendent. Whatever helps Old souls do that is likely to become a favorite pastime.

When Old souls do involve themselves in groups, it's usually around something that interests them and fulfills their need for community and connection. They don't bother with superficial relationships but enjoy simple gatherings of close friends and quiet evenings of conversation. Old souls rarely while away the hours with games like cards that just fill up time, except occasionally to accommodate others and fit in socially.

SEXUALITY

Although Infant souls are afraid of almost everything, sex is not one of them. This is probably because they live close to their instincts, and sexuality is largely instinctual. As a result, Infant souls aren't discriminating about partners or loyal to one partner. This changes significantly by the Baby cycle, when we begin to respond to the rules laid down by family and society and begin to view our sexuality with suspicion and shame.

The mutual dependency of the Baby cycle makes intimacy tantamount to survival. Baby souls are aware that their survival may depend on how they conduct themselves in their personal relationships, so Baby souls do their best to curtail their sex drive if it might interfere with meeting their other needs. So while Infant souls rely on others to help them control their sex drive, Baby souls control it themselves if that is the social norm.

Baby souls still aren't good at choosing partners. They usually attract other Baby souls, who also want partnerships based on fulfilling basic needs, such as food, shelter, safety, and sex. Companionship, which is so important in later cycles, is rarely a priority in the intimate relationships of Baby souls. Shared interests are not even necessary. The marriages of Baby souls are marriages of convenience. Nevertheless, these relationships begin the process of learning to love. Baby souls at least show some loyalty in their relationships, in contrast to Infant souls, who have little interest in relationships at all.

Sexual attraction is a major factor in drawing people together in any cycle, but in no other cycle is it more of a basis for relationship than in the Young cycle. In this cycle, sexual attractiveness is the measure of whether someone is acceptable or not. Survival considerations are no longer what determines the choice of mate. Young souls want partners who add to their assets. To them, physical beauty is intrinsically valuable and worthy of love regardless of other attributes. Young souls are superficial, although they don't think of themselves this way but as connoisseurs of beauty. Unfortunately, Young souls who aren't beautiful live in considerable pain, but they do learn to appreciate the value of other attributes as a result. Still, it isn't until the end of this cycle that Young souls strive to develop these other attributes.

In the Mature cycle, the emphasis is on intelligence, talent, competence, and other qualities besides physical beauty. Physical appearance is still usually the basis for initial evaluation, though. What changes in this cycle is that the standard for beauty is broader. What Mature souls consider beautiful, Young souls might not.

Unlike in earlier cycles, Mature souls see their sexuality as just one facet of themselves, and not the most important one either. They feel that flaunting their sexuality and using it to manipulate others is crass and unseemly. Mature souls feel they are beyond this, priding themselves in their sexual control and modesty. In fact, sexual repression is common in this cycle. Mature souls feel shame around sexuality, just as Baby souls do. So it seems that Young souls react against the repression of the Baby cycle, and Mature souls react against the provocativeness of the Young cycle.

Some Old souls identify so little with their sexuality that they're comfortable with long periods of celibacy, although this hardly characterizes all Old souls. Most Old souls take their sexuality in stride as another interesting aspect of themselves without giving it much importance or energy. For them, sexuality is something pleasurable that can enhance their relationships and bring them a greater awareness of Spirit.

Many Old souls are interested in how sexual energy can be transmuted, and they may experiment with kundalini yoga, celibacy, and tantric sex to achieve the spiritual union they long for. By the very end of this cycle, sexual relations are often of little interest, and many discontinue having sex entirely. This isn't because Old souls think sex detracts from a spiritual life, but because they feel that sex doesn't have anything to offer them.

Those who fight to tame their sexuality early in the Old cycle are anticipating the course that this cycle eventually takes, but avoiding sexual relations isn't necessary to our spiritual evolution. For some, celibacy is a natural outgrowth of this cycle. Attempts to be celibate before it comes naturally may not be helpful.

CHAPTER 6
Soul Age and Relationships

Many things affect the dynamics between two people: upbringing, experiences, age, gender, religion, culture, appearance, intelligence, education, social class, political beliefs, race, sexual orientation, and physical ability. Less obvious things, such as soul age, the horoscope, and past-life experiences, often go unacknowledged but are also important. In fact, sometimes, our behavior, fears, perceptions, preferences, and needs can *only* be explained by these more esoteric and obscure factors. Once these other influences are commonly recognized, we'll understand our relationships—and ourselves—much better.

Soul age explains some of the differences between people, like why two children brought up in the same family may respond very differently to life. Soul age may even explain the form a relationship takes, such as the role-reversal between parent and child we sometimes see. In these cases, the child might be an older soul than the parent. Understanding this influence is helpful in handling this important aspect of our lives.

FAMILY RELATIONSHIPS

The family is the primary social unit. It is also the arena in which many of the lessons of evolution are learned. From the soul's perspective, families present an opportunity to bring people together for many years who might not ordinarily choose to be together. The soul often puts people together who challenge each other to grow in ways they need to grow. Family members have to find a way to coexist regardless of their differences—or suffer. Within our families, we have a chance to improve our relationship skills and experience close up what different people are like.

Several patterns emerge when we look at family relationships from the standpoint of soul age. One is a family composed of younger souls with one child who is an Old soul. Each family member learns something from this arrangement. The Old soul child grows up sensing that he or she is different, which mirrors reality outside the family and helps the child adjust to this reality. And the family bond makes it easier for the Old soul child to accept and understand younger souls in general, which is one of the lessons of the Old cycle. The same is true for the Old soul's siblings, who find it easier to accept their "odd" sibling than if he or she were a stranger. The parents benefit by learning to be more open-minded and by experiencing a new level of love from their Old soul child.

When an Old soul is the child of much younger souls, there may be a karmic debt owed to the child by one or both parents. Although we're never required to be present for a karmic atonement if it might incur more pain, which is always a possibility, many Old souls agree to this, knowing the challenge will accelerate their growth. So the younger soul may choose this situation as an opportunity to repay a debt, while the Old soul may choose it for its potential for growth.

Another common pattern in families is Old soul parents with younger soul children. When this happens, it's often because the Old souls have chosen to be teachers to the younger ones. The younger souls benefit because the positive environment that the Old soul parents provide develops the potentials and ability to love of the younger souls or helps them heal from a previous trauma. Although younger soul children are bound to be a challenge even to Old soul parents, those parents have the resources to deal with this challenge. And on some level, if not consciously, the Old souls even welcome it.

One of the more common family patterns is younger soul children with Mature soul parents. The purposes are similar to those for combining younger soul children with Old soul parents except that this arrangement is made equally for the Mature souls' growth. The stress presented by such a challenge fosters the psychological and emotional growth so important to the Mature cycle. Motivated by the parental bond, Mature souls try to understand these children and, in so doing, learn to accept younger souls.

While Old souls are more likely to serve Mature or other Old souls through service projects or their work, Mature souls often work with younger souls, especially when they have younger soul children themselves. Younger souls benefit from the sensitivity, understanding, and insight of Mature souls. So one remedy for the superficiality and selfishness of the Young cycle is having Mature soul parents, counselors, or teachers.

Unlike Old souls, Mature souls aren't often placed with younger soul parents because of the Mature soul's sensitivity and the lessons of the Mature cycle. Mature soul children are easily hurt by younger soul adults, who can be insensitive to the Mature soul's emotional needs. Besides, Mature soul children need insight into their feelings and needs, which is rarely available from younger soul parents.

When Mature souls are placed with younger soul parents, it's usually because the Mature soul owes a debt to the younger soul parent. Sometimes debts of this nature are repaid in the Mature soul's later years by caring for the aging parent. The sensitivity and compassion of Mature souls enable them to give to others even when these relationships aren't particularly rewarding for them.

Another fairly common family arrangement is Old soul parents with Mature soul children. Because these parents can further their children's psychological understanding, this is ideal for Mature soul children. The only problem is that this arrangement may not provide the level of challenge that can be so productive within families. Consequently, this arrangement is chosen only when everyone can benefit from this more than from something more challenging or when a Mature soul needs healing. For that matter, anyone who needs healing, regardless of soul age, might be given to Old soul parents.

The family serves many functions. It conveys religious and societal values, protects and nurtures, and teaches practical skills and how to live with others. In considering the effectiveness with which a family functions, we also need to consider how the soul ages of its members relate to the soul age of the society or community in which that family functions. Soul age not only affects the amount of conflict within a family, but also the amount of conflict a family experiences with those outside the family.

In the United States, families with predominantly Baby or Young souls are less conflicted about values, since their values mirror the society in which they live. The same can't be said for families in which the predominant soul age is Mature or Old. This disparity in values causes these older souls some confusion and discomfort. They're likely to feel outside the mainstream of society, which can affect how they feel about themselves and how well they function within society. The children, in particular, may long for parents with values like their peers and feel inferior to others their age. But after these children mature, they're likely to feel differently, eschewing the values they once emulated.

Families with predominantly Baby or Young souls have other problems. They aren't likely to communicate effectively or handle their feelings constructively. They also allow each other less freedom to be themselves. So although they may be under less pressure from society, their members are under greater pressure to conform to the desires of other family members than families composed of Mature or Old souls.

Many families are composed of a variety of soul ages. In these families, major barriers to communication and understanding and conflicts about values are likely. The stress is greatest when the difference in soul ages is more than one cycle because the perceptions are so far apart. So families with both

Infant or Baby souls and Mature or Old souls are bound to have major differences, creating considerable pain for their members.

In general, the greater the gap in soul age, the greater the misunderstandings. This is less true when Old souls are involved because of their higher level of acceptance and understanding. When conflict is great, a family might have difficulty performing its function. Consequently, families with diverse soul ages are more likely to be dysfunctional than more homogeneous families. The dysfunction is usually aggravated if the youngest souls are in the parental role.

Families composed mostly of Young, Mature, or Old souls with one member unlike the others may function fairly well. In these families, whoever is different is likely to be cited as the problem and pressured to change. This is a strain on the whole family, but more so on the scapegoat. The remaining family members are likely to function smoothly in their shared perceptions if they don't conflict too greatly with the values of their society or those around them, such as neighbors, relatives, or community members.

The soul often brings the same people together as family members repeatedly because this has many advantages. Frequently, two people reincarnate in the same family in two different lifetimes in opposite roles. This can occur in any of the three possible dyads: parent/child, husband/wife, or brother/sister. The former child becomes the parent and the former parent becomes the child, with the same switching occurring in the other dyads.

Sometimes the people in one family keep switching roles in future families until every role of each dyad is experienced by each of them. By doing this, we come to understand the function our roles play in our perceptions. Strong karmic bonds are formed from sharing many lifetimes in these close family relationships, some positive and some not.

A *karmic bond* refers to the feeling between two people who are learning, have learned, or will learn something important from each other or who are contributing, have contributed, or will contribute to each other's lives in some significant way. If we take the term *karmic relationship* to mean a relationship that has a purpose that is decided before life, then family relationships are nearly always karmic.

Not every family member has a karmic bond with every other family member, of course, but each member is likely to have at least one karmic bond with one other person in the family. As a result, the family system is often divided into groupings, factions, or special alliances. This is no surprise to family therapists, who study these alliances, although the reason for these alliances is often a mystery to family therapists.

ROMANTIC RELATIONSHIPS

Romance usually happens between people of the same soul age. Occasionally, romantic partners are one cycle apart, but these relationships are often unsatisfactory for one or both people and usually have a karmic basis, most likely some kind of karmic debt. The soul sometimes uses physical attraction to bring two people together who might not ordinarily choose to be together, especially when there's been some difficulty in a former lifetime between them.

Although people aren't required to return to a relationship to balance a debt, those involved often choose to because it's the most effective way for both to learn. When two people decide before life that they will meet again to balance a karmic debt, sexual attraction is often used to draw them together and keep them together until the debt is balanced, if that's feasible. Besides sexual attraction, these relationships have a sense of obligation or compulsion about them for at least one if not both of the individuals.

Most relationships of a karmic nature take place when one or both of the individuals are in the Young or Mature cycles, even though the offenses probably occurred in the Infant or Baby cycles. Sometimes the balancing is begun earlier, but most debts are balanced in the Young and Mature cycles, when we have the resources and will to make amends and are unlikely to repeat the mistake. Because it can take several lifetimes to pay a karmic debt, some debts aren't completely paid until the Old cycle.

Although it may seem ludicrous to try to balance a karmic debt between a Young soul and an Old one via a romantic relationship, this isn't as implausible as it sounds. Many Young souls are wealthy, since money and power relate to their lessons, and that enables them to benefit others financially. As a result, Young souls often marry Old or Mature souls to repay a karmic debt. Besides, the marriage may not even have to endure for the debt to be paid.

Many who are in difficult relationships assume they have to stay in them, sensing that karma is involved. But this isn't necessarily true. The presence of karma between two people isn't always enough reason to stay together. Sometimes the karma can't be balanced within the existing circumstances. When the soul arranges for two people to meet, fall in love, and balance a karmic debt, no one knows if it will work as intended. Sometimes, because of the soul's miscalculations, free will, or other reasons, the karma can't be balanced or balanced completely. In that case, it may be best for the two to abandon their attempts and try again in another lifetime. Some of the most miserable couples are those who don't end their commitment to each other when their souls have, at least for that particular lifetime.

Those in difficult relationships often wonder whether they should leave it or keep working at it. Every situation is unique, or course, but here are some guidelines: First, is the situation physically or emotionally abusive? If it is, it will only incur more karma if the abuse continues. The lesson for the abused is to refuse to be abused, which is accomplished by leaving the abuser. The lesson for the abuser is that abuse causes loved ones to leave. Second, can the individuals grow and fulfill their souls' plans within the relationship? If a relationship prohibits either from growing and having a fulfilling life, remaining together isn't a good choice. And third, is the relationship creating an environment of hatred, resentment, and anger? If so, it's best to abandon the relationship. However, sometimes through therapy, other healing methods, or spiritual work, such negative feelings can be overcome, and that growth might be very important to the individuals.

Karmic debts between two people of very different soul ages are the hardest to balance. Vast differences in soul age make bringing two people into loving relationship difficult, since shared perceptions are lacking. When this is the situation, sexual attraction may not be enough. In these cases, the souls of the individuals are likely to use a familial relationship rather than a romantic one to bring and keep the two people together long enough to balance a debt.

Fortunately, our romantic relationships are not all karmic. Some are freely entered into out of genuine love and respect, often developed through romantic relationships, friendships, or familial relationships in former lifetimes. Any positive experience with another in a previous lifetime may lead to a later attraction. Whether or not that attraction develops into something more depends on the same factors that determine the dynamics in every relationship. If we had a romantic relationship in a former lifetime with someone, the chances of this recurring are great if other factors don't override it.

When two people meet lifetime after lifetime and share a deepening of love on each occasion, these individuals are often called *soul mates*. Soul mate relationships usually begin as other kinds of relationships and develop into romantic relationships only later. In soul mate relationships, there's a sense of deep love and commitment, especially if their former relationships involved close family ties. The relationship of parent and child is a particularly strong one and common in the background of soul mates. But this doesn't mean that a parent/child relationship will develop into a soul mate relationship without other ingredients.

The main difference between soul mate relationships and karmic ones is that soul mate relationships are freely chosen for exploring and developing love. They nearly always are between two people who are not only in the same cycle, but also in the same or nearly the same place in that cycle, since shared perceptions and lessons make for greater compatibility and understanding. In some long-standing soul mate relationships, the two individuals have progressed at a similar pace through several cycles in relationship after relationship.

When does a relationship become a soul mate relationship? If we could agree on the answer to this, the term wouldn't be so confusing. Even one positive romantic relationship may be enough to deserve this label. But that would leave each of us with many soul mates. Obviously, this kind of soul mate relationship and one that has endured for centuries aren't equal.

Some soul mate relationships don't endure beyond a few lifetimes, but those that do are powerful and unmistakable to the two involved. In ones that endure, a sense of belonging and a deep level of trust are common, even before that trust is earned. These relationships are easy, comfortable, and smooth compared to others. Of course, something else that contributes to this ease is that most people in soul mate relationships are Old souls, who already know how to communicate well and love deeply.

OTHER RELATIONSHIPS

Because it underlies compatibility and mutual understanding, soul age affects all our relationships, even our less significant ones. Many of our relationships outside the family involve working with others in groups: in classrooms, in church groups, in political organizations, in the community, on athletic teams, and in the workplace. Groups composed of several soul ages or even just two very different ones are likely to have their productivity limited by conflict. Furthermore, the tasks that a group is willing and capable of taking on depend on the soul ages of its members.

Certain kinds of groups appeal to certain soul ages. Health clubs, for instance, appeal to Young souls because health clubs cater to physical strength and beauty, so valued by Young souls. Although political organizations appeal to a wide range of soul ages, each political faction is likely to be composed of people of a similar soul age, with each ideology reflecting the perspective of that soul age. The same can be said about religious organizations, which appeal to souls of all ages, but whose specific doctrines appeal to certain individuals according to their perceptions.

Some of the hardest groups within which to operate are ones composed of many different soul ages, such as neighborhood and community groups and places of employment. In these organizations, a hierarchy is usually established to facilitate the group's goals, since the group can't be expected to function on consensus. Different structures are appropriate for different kinds of groups, depending in part on whether or not the group is homogeneous in soul age.

Even homogeneous groups may vary greatly in effectiveness depending on the appropriateness of the group's task to its majority soul age. For instance, a group of Young souls would have difficulty putting together a task force on alcoholism or runaway teens because they aren't likely to understand the issues or be motivated to do this. Community action such as this is usually headed and carried out by Mature or Old souls, whose life purposes and interests are in keeping with such a project. Putting the wrong people in charge of certain tasks is one explanation for the inefficiency in government programs.

Working together with others is never easy. Even in the best of circumstances, when people are the same soul age and working at tasks appropriate to their soul age, personality conflicts and differences are bound to arise. But the conflict generated by personality differences can't compare to that generated by differences in soul age. Each soul age sees life through its own pair of glasses. Different soul ages just don't see life the same way.

PART 2

How Karma Works and Traumas Are Healed

CHAPTER 7
Near Deaths and Traumatic Deaths

BRUSHES WITH DEATH

This chapter explores how the soul heals the trauma of serious accidents and violence. Close brushes with death are nearly always traumatizing. The importance of what happens following a scrape with death will be evident in the following stories. How an incident and its effects are handled determines how traumatized someone will be. But this isn't all that affects how a traumatic experience is internalized. The victim's astrology chart, previous experiences (including past-life experiences), gender, and age are also significant in shaping the victim's reactions to the event. All of these influence what psychological adaptations the victim makes.

Case A

This is the story of a girl named Alana who was brutally raped and left bleeding to die many lifetimes ago. Alana fought her attacker until she no longer had the strength and then fell unconscious. Her attacker left her for dead and escaped.

Very early the next morning, Alana was discovered by a

traveler on the road where her attacker had left her. The traveler loaded her into his wagon, took her to a nearby house, and summoned a physician. After bandaging her, Alana was taken to her home, where she lived alone with her frail and somewhat elderly mother.

Her mother didn't ask any questions. She had seen this kind of thing before and thought it was improper to speak about it. She attended to her daughter meticulously, as she would anything that required her attention, but they never spoke about what happened.

Alana was thirteen years old and had never been with a man before. She felt terrified, confused, and alone. She saw no future for herself because she couldn't imagine ever being with a man after that. Unfortunately, Alana never knew her father, who had left her mother shortly after her birth, and there were no other men in her life to reshape her ideas about men. She lived only a few more years, succumbing to an illness common then.

Her next incarnation took into account her need for healing. Her astrology chart emphasized the element of fire to give her the independence, fortitude, and assertiveness to heal this issue. Her family named her Greta. This family was loving and large, one where nothing was too private or sacred to be discussed and where the parents were openly affectionate. And, Greta was attractive. The plan was obvious: to create circumstances in which romantic love could flower.

Although Greta's environment lived up to her soul's intentions, she still suffered as a result of the experience in her previous lifetime. Despite Greta's fiery astrology chart, she was shy and withdrawn and had trouble sharing her thoughts. She was different from the rest of her family, but they accepted her and encouraged her to be more confident. Nevertheless, to fulfill her potentials, she would have to overcome her pain. There were no psychotherapists, shamans, witches, or other healers in her country, only priests. This left the healing up to those in her environment—and her soul.

One day while sitting alone in a secluded spot on a hill, Greta had the sensation of being totally free and unfettered. She sensed she could do anything, that she could do something important. This was the first time she'd thought about anything other than her day-to-day existence and the possibility of marriage and a family.

As this sense within her grew, Greta was led to a family who had a daughter around her own age who was paralyzed. Greta visited the girl daily and read to her. One day, she was reading her a story about a dancer, and the girl began to cry. The paralyzed girl would never know what it was like to dance. This touched Greta and strengthened her appreciation for her own freedom and vitality. Circumstances were working to draw out Greta's fiery energy.

Greta married. Her husband was a warm and loving man, robust and affectionate, much like her own father. But she had difficulty adjusting to the sexual aspect of their marriage. For some reason that she didn't understand, intimacy felt frightening and shameful to her. Nevertheless, with her husband's gentle encouragement and sensitivity, she learned to be more relaxed and trusting. She began to blossom as she saw her children grow into happy, free-spirited individuals.

Despite Greta's busy life, deep feelings of compassion moved her to visit the hospital regularly, where she chatted with the patients and shared her cheery disposition. Her shyness mellowed into a warm receptivity to the pain of others, and her friendliness and optimism gave others hope and eased their suffering. She realized she had a gift for helping others, which she used throughout the remainder of that lifetime.

In her next lifetime, she was a woman again. One more step was necessary to heal the wound inflicted lifetimes ago. The rape hadn't been part of her soul's plan then but interfered with it, which is why her soul left her body early through illness. The plan for this lifetime would be to recreate the situation, but with a favorable outcome. Her soul would try to arrange a situation in which her protests would release her from her attacker. Fighting back hadn't helped her before and resulted in feelings of helplessness. To increase the likelihood of success, her environment, astrology chart, and early experiences were carefully chosen.

This time, when the attack happened, she succeeded in freeing herself from her attacker, balancing her sense of helplessness. After this, she began helping other rape victims. This lifetime, instead of being one of victimization, became one of service and strength. She had come through this ordeal with greater compassion, fortitude, and faith in the human spirit.

Although we may not be able to understand the meaning of events as they are happening, every event eventually leads to good. What's hard for us to accept is that the good may not be apparent until other lifetimes. From an earthly standpoint, this is undeniably unfair. But from the soul's standpoint, not only is life fair, but also something we have willingly and eagerly entered into.

Case B

A boy named Daniel was fishing from the side of a river one day with a friend. He was trying to get to another fishing spot on the other side of the river when the current dragged him under. After being swept downstream a short distance, he resurfaced, where he grabbed a log and rode it to safety. In the meantime, his friend, who had gone for help, returned with two men and a rope. Daniel was resting on the bank just downstream. With hoots of gladness, they called and waved to him. He felt particularly alive; he'd escaped death. In school, everyone was interested in hearing about his misadventure, which made him feel like a hero. This event made a deep impression on him. He saw himself as a survivor, someone who comes out on top.

His next lifetime was as a female named Mary. Even as a child, Mary was bold and confident. Although her astrology chart didn't reflect this particularly, she exuded a rare confidence and self-satisfaction.

Mary lived in a small village where women and girls were expected to do the domestic tasks while the men hunted, farmed, and provided in other ways. She was restless and discontent. She longed to be special. One day while helping her father with chores in the barn, one of the animals kicked over a lantern and started a fire, which spread quickly. Mary grabbed a bucket of milk nearby and flung it, which dampened the blaze just enough to control it. At last, she had the admiration she longed for. Her subconscious belief in her ability to come out on top was reinforced.

In her next lifetime, the plan was to continue to develop her bravery and sense of mastery. So her soul chose a male incarnation, circumstances that would demand courage and enterprise, and an astrology chart conducive to developing these qualities. Billy was the given name in this incarnation. Billy was born into a family that captured and broke wild mustangs. He loved going with his father to track, rope, and bring in the mustangs.

One day while riding alone, Billy spotted a mountain lion sunning on a rock. He stopped, dismounted, tied his horse, and quietly climbed toward the lion, trying to get a closer look at it without it seeing him. The mountain lion caught his scent and charged. Billy didn't escape without a terrible swipe from its paws, gouging him across his arm. The mountain lion retreated, leaving Billy alone with his bleeding arm. Using his shirt as a bandage, he managed to get home.

When Billy arrived home, he was scolded, but also joyfully embraced. For some, this experience might have resulted in self-doubt or unconscious fears, but topping other successful brushes with death in former lifetimes, it contributed to this individual's sense of mastery and invincibility. At this point, the soul may either continue to create experiences to develop courage and fearlessness or just find ways to use the courage the individual already has.

TRAUMATIC DEATHS

Traumatic deaths can be more psychologically damaging for the loved ones who survive than for the one who has died, especially if the loved ones have witnessed the death. Nevertheless, traumatic deaths often leave the one who died with emotional scars that will need to be addressed in future lifetimes.

The extent of the damage and what will be needed to heal it depend on the circumstances and the individual's development. Of greatest importance is the state of mind at death. It helps if the individual found some inner peace and acceptance before death. If he or she died with strong feelings of fear, regret, anger, or sorrow, the assumptions underlying these feelings will need healing.

Healing a traumatic death nearly always entails working with the underlying beliefs about oneself or about life reflected in the prominent feeling at death. These beliefs and feelings are influenced by the individual's astrology chart and all previous experiences. The importance of the state of mind at death will be obvious in the stories that follow.

Some healing also occurs between lifetimes on the astral plane. We are offered instruction, guidance, and healing when we arrive on the astral plane, which prepare us for further healing on the physical plane. How effective this is depends on our willingness to be helped.

When considerable damage has occurred or if we are refusing help, we may sit out the dance of life for what would amount to several lifetimes before we feel ready to face another ordinary life of challenges or one designed for healing.

As an alternative to sitting it out on the astral plane, we might choose a lifetime of ease. This is possible because the soul can block out wounds if that's advantageous. It does this by giving a directive to the unconscious to block recognition of the psychological effects of a particular incident. Although this is only a temporary measure to provide some relief from psychological pain, it can help build some psychological strength and distance from the offense, making healing in later lifetimes easier.

The following stories show how a traumatic death or the trauma from witnessing one might be healed.

Case C

A young boy named Ton-Ton was walking in the woods one day when he came upon a trap meant for a large animal. Inside it lay a man who was broken, bleeding, and gasping for his last breaths.

Ton-Ton was too small to help the man, so he did the only thing he could think of: He cried for help. Being very young, he didn't think of running to get help, but stayed there crying. He continued to intermittently call for help and cry tearfully. Finally, at about the same time a party of hunters found the distraught child, the man gave up his life.

If Ton-Ton had been older, he probably would have had the emotional resources to cope with the trauma and the intellectual wherewithal to have taken more effective action. As it was, he felt responsible for the death, and a sense of shame and guilt haunted him the rest of that lifetime.

To help him work through this, in his next lifetime, his soul would try to arrange for him to save someone's life, although trying to heal something this way is risky. An opportunity may never arrive or a lack of confidence may interfere with success. Selecting the right environment and astrology chart was crucial. Having done this, it was up to his soul to try to arrange the right circumstances.

The opportunity arose when he was in the military. In a battle one day, he had the opportunity to save several men. He did manage to save one person but was deeply regretful over not saving the others. Fortunately, he was able to discuss his feelings with others who'd had a similar experience. He even received a medal for his heroism. And his adult reason told him he wasn't responsible for the deaths of the others.

All this helped, but subtle feelings of guilt lingered on. To cope with these feelings, he established a support group for surviving soldiers. So his own need for healing gave birth to a means for healing many. He'd found a way to continue his own healing and to transform his pain into understanding. He grew in compassion not only for others, but more importantly, also for himself. And with this compassion came forgiveness, the last step in the healing process.

Case D

This is the story of a man named Alexander who was tortured to death. As much as we'd like it to be otherwise, torture has been a constant throughout history. As long as humankind is ruled by the ego, such acts will persist.

What effect does an incident like torture have on someone's psyche? There is no one answer to this. Everyone internalizes experiences differently and in more ways than one. This death reinforced Alexander's conviction that his integrity was more precious than his life and that he was more than just his body. But Alexander also internalized a sense of fatalism, which he brought into his next lifetime. It's difficult to come away from a tortured death without some sense of futility and some loss of faith in the goodness of humankind. In the scope of each lifetime, the good don't always win, and we can't help but be affected by this.

Alexander's next lifetime would be one that would allow him to express the compassion he'd gained from his tragic death and continue his spiritual goal of service. Although the tortuous death didn't prevent him from serving others in his next lifetime, it did prevent him from enjoying life more fully. A sense of futility overwhelmed him. Since service without joy is closer to servitude than true service, he needed something to reactivate his joy and appreciation of life's blessedness.

In his next lifetime, his soul chose an astrology chart that supported fun, creativity, courage, and self-expression (Leo). It also provided circumstances of relative luxury, which freed him from the stress of survival and gave him opportunities for self-expression and pleasure.

Although he wasn't attuned to this playful, courageous, and creative energy, these energies still worked their magic on him. He gained a sense of control and mastery over life, which counteracted his former feelings of futility and powerlessness. Out of gratitude for his good fortune, he founded a school for unfortunate children that instilled spiritual values and gave the children opportunities for creative expression. This lifetime balanced his sense of futility, expanded his repertoire of behaviors, and equipped him to serve in a wider variety of ways than before.

Case E

While walking alone one day, Karen came across a man who'd been run over by a train. The sight was the biggest shock of her life. She became physically ill but managed to get herself back home and notify the authorities. Even though she didn't know the man and felt no responsibility for his death, it affected her deeply. At twenty, Karen's life was just beginning. Her own death seemed remote until this reminder.

Karen responded to this tragedy by searching for a belief system that would help her be more comfortable with the uncertainty of life. Eventually, she discovered beliefs that brought comfort to her and helped her bring comfort to others too. This resolved any negative effects this experience might have had on her.

Every experience, whether chosen for us by our souls or not, has the potential to further our growth and enrich our lives. The result of any experience depends on our responses to it—the choices we make. Whatever the choice, it will lead to growth, but some choices lead us more gracefully to this than others. There is no blame in any of our choices. We are here to learn. Whether we make satisfying choices or painful ones, the outcome is eventually greater understanding.

Let's go back and look at this story from the victim's standpoint. He was also young, about the same age as Karen. He was walking from one town to the next along the railroad tracks when he decided he'd make better time if he hopped a train. He waited at a curve where the train would be traveling more slowly. Had he known better, he would have realized that this was extremely dangerous and likely to fail. When his opportunity came, he jumped, lost his grip, and fell under the train's wheels.

Because this young man's death was so immediate, we might think it had little effect on his psyche, but at the moment of death, the mind takes in the entire experience and draws conclusions. In one split second, he recognized his folly and concluded that he had poor judgment. He carried this conclusion into his next lifetime.

In the lifetime that followed, he was careful and somewhat fearful. People said he was sensible and practical, characteristics that resulted from his former death and an astrology chart with plenty of Capricorn. His tragic death had taught him to be more cautious, and the careful choices he'd make in this lifetime would teach him that he could trust his judgment. By the end of this lifetime, his distrust in himself would be balanced and he would be wiser. In his next lifetime, he's likely to act with common sense—and confidence.

We all have made similar mistakes in our past lives. Experiences like these teach us caution, common sense, and responsibility. We aren't born knowing these things; we have to learn them. Losing our life over something as seemingly preventable as poor judgment is never easy, but such incidents are part of life's lessons.

Death is an unknown. Not only do we not know what lies on the other side of death, but many of us believe more pain and retribution await us, if anything at all. These attitudes don't make death any easier. Our beliefs about death affect our state of mind before death. And as we have seen, this state determines what beliefs we carry into our next lifetime.

Although some people don't fear death, they are in the minority. Most of us need some understanding about death and support at death to make this transition successfully. A lack of preparation for death can make not only leaving life more difficult, but also entering into new life in other realms difficult. Fortunately, we're beginning to realize the importance of preparing people for death when that's possible.

Death is always successful. No one has ever been unsuccessful in shedding his or her body. But dying successfully in another sense means coming to peace with our death. There comes a time when we learn to die more consciously, when we know we are more than the ego, more than the experience of death, and more than the perspective held at death.

This realization comes to people at different points in their evolution, usually in the Old cycle. When the time comes, the soul often designs a method of death to bring about this realization. When death isn't actively engaged in teaching us a lesson, such as better judgment, the soul might use our death to make us more aware of our spiritual nature. The lessons of life are many, and some are taught through death. Oddly enough, death is also a way of teaching us about our immortality.

CHAPTER 8
Traumatic Accidents

The psychological impact of traumatic accidents is similar to that of traumatic deaths, except that the individual faces the need for healing in that same lifetime. Unfortunately, sometimes the psychological effects of an accident become more entrenched rather than healed, and the remainder of the victim's life is seen through the distorted lens of his or her victimization.

What's most important to psychological healing are the victim's attitude and willingness to recommit to life following an accident. The victim has to be willing to see the future as worthwhile. This shift in attitude *is* the healing in many cases and may even be the reason for the accident. Our attitude affects not only our capacity to heal, but also the amount of psychological damage that results from an accident. Negative conclusions formed at the time of an accident can have a long-term psychological impact, just as those formed at the moment of death. If the victim continues to hold those beliefs, they may become limiting and self-fulfilling. The stories that follow illustrate these points.

Case F

Lynn lost her young child and sustained serious injuries to her face and body in an automobile accident. Her only thought then was for her young daughter, who died instantly. Because Lynn hadn't been able to prevent her daughter's death, she felt responsible, even though there was nothing she could have done. As a result, Lynn's mind became fixed on her daughter's death rather than on her own recovery. Lynn's mood became despondent, slowing her progress in physical therapy and dampening her motivation to have plastic surgery. She didn't care about living, even though she had a loving husband, a son, and the potential for full recovery.

When these tragedies happen, people understandably wonder why. There is no one answer to this question. In this instance, both Lynn and her child had chosen this experience before birth. But not every accident is prearranged; some are accidents. Even when an accident isn't part of our spiritual plan, our soul can usually find a way to use it for good.

For Lynn, the accident was to be a way of counteracting her frivolousness and vanity. Because Lynn valued appearances too much, her soul designed this accident to help her realize the value of life beyond appearances. Such tragedies help us see that who we really are remains unchanged and what has changed is not really who we are.

The child, on the other hand, joined this family to further the family members' compassion and to advance her own understanding by dying this way. Early death is a lesson we all have to face. As difficult as it may be to see any benefit in a child dying, such a death does increase that soul's appreciation of life and motivation to live. As a result, early death is sometimes chosen to prevent a recurrence of suicide when someone has committed suicide in the past.

As might be expected, Lynn was angry and disheartened for some time. As she watched her body heal, she regretted losing her beauty and longed to be beautiful again. It took years before she accepted her fate and decided to get on with life in her new body. She began by getting involved with an after-school project for disadvantaged youths, which gave her an outlet for expressing the love she had inside her. If she couldn't share her love with her lost child, she would share it with other children. In her next lifetime, she's likely to continue to serve in some way, using the compassion and understanding she developed from this experience.

Life is never easy. But at times we do see our life with clarity, and it shines with meaning. Just because this state isn't constant doesn't mean that life lacks meaning, only that this vision is hard to sustain. Sometimes it takes a tragedy to awaken our search for meaning and open us to the soul's wisdom. Once we begin searching for the answer to, "Why me?" we're often led in unexpected and meaningful directions.

The wisdom and growth garnered from traumatic experiences can't be gained from books or even from others. Experience teaches life's lessons like no amount of study can. If you look back on your life, you're likely to see that your greatest strengths have come from your greatest challenges. This is how wisdom is born, and no other way. Wisdom is a jewel born from pain.

Case G

Jan lost his arm in a farm accident. He was only ten then and didn't have the emotional resources or family support to deal successfully with this loss. He concluded that his life would never be normal. If the accident had happened later in his life, he might not have felt that his condition was so limiting.

This belief became a self-fulfilling prophecy, as do many negative beliefs. Jan's feelings of inferiority affected other areas of his life and became more handicapping than the disability itself. Others began seeing him as incapable too and compensated for him, reinforcing his sense of inferiority. After all, if others do things for us, not only do we not learn to do these things for ourselves, but we may also question our capability. Those who work with the handicapped know this because many of them were disabled in former lifetimes. Many who are now handicapped know this too from other lifetimes and have chosen to be disabled again to act as models for others.

At the end of this lifetime, Jan needed healing for the trauma he'd suffered and for a lifetime of unmet potential and feelings of inferiority. In his next lifetime, his soul chose a family that would help him develop his confidence and talents. This family had the material and emotional resources to give him a strong sense of self-worth and the ease he needed to recuperate from his previous lifetime.

With this as his foundation, he ventured into athletics. Physical prowess was something he'd developed in other lifetimes. His soul would use this and an appropriate astrology chart to rebuild his confidence. This lifetime built his physical prowess and psychic strength, which prepared him to face the lessons of disability again in his next lifetime.

For that lifetime, his soul chose another supportive family and, this time, an accident in which he lost his leg. The tragedy happened in his teenage years, just when he was beginning to excel in team sports. His love of sports carried him through this injury because he wanted so badly to participate in sports again. Every day he worked to build his strength so that he could support himself on one leg. Eventually, he developed a means of mobility that allowed him to run and compete in certain games. He would never be a professional athlete or excel as he might have, but he grew to be grateful for what he could do—and he never stopped dreaming of what he might achieve.

You may be wondering why Jan found himself in a situation initially that wasn't conducive to meeting the challenge of losing his arm. Could it have been part of his plan to lose his arm at age ten and not have a supportive family? Does the soul ever set us up for failure? The answer is no.

The soul never chooses circumstances that are impossible to handle. When challenges are chosen, it's always with the belief that they can be used for growth. If circumstances turn out to be overwhelming, it's usually because someone has interfered with the plan. Since the soul is unable to control the choices of others, sometimes a situation is created that's unexpected and unprepared for. When that happens, we have to make the best of it and learn whatever we can from it. Even these situations have their value, if not only to teach us greater patience, perseverance, and compassion. So every challenge leads to learning of some sort, which can usually be used for good in future lifetimes if not immediately.

Losing his arm wasn't part of Jan's plan. As a result, the soul's initial plan had to be set aside. If his soul had decided that it was impossible to work within these circumstances, it would have left the body, but his soul saw a potential for advancement through these new circumstances. Just because Jan didn't advance doesn't mean he couldn't have or that his soul wasn't trying to help him. Unfortunately, the soul's tactics don't always work.

Case H

Jack became paralyzed after a fall. Although the paralysis wasn't initially part of his plan, it became part of his plan later. His soul created this accident to shift Jack's focus away from physical development, which was interfering with accomplishing his life purpose. Before life, Jack's soul and three others had agreed to collaborate on an invention, but Jack's exceptional athletic abilities were sidetracking him. To bring Jack's focus back to his life purpose, his soul brought about the fall that caused his paralysis.

Although this way of steering Jack's plan may seem drastic, his soul had other motives for this choice. Jack had become callous toward those who couldn't perform as well as him athletically. We often expect others to have equal abilities, not realizing that our talents come from lifetimes of development. The paralysis balanced this callousness and developed his compassion.

If his soul had felt that its goals couldn't be accomplished this way, other tactics would've been used or that particular life purpose abandoned and replaced by one related to his physical skills. There are always many options. But, knowing that Jack had the inner strength and astrology chart to support mental accomplishments, not just physical ones, his soul chose this plan.

Case I

Barry sustained a brain injury when he fell from a window. The trauma left him temporarily unable to speak or write, although he could understand what was said to him. This accident had been planned before life to accomplish two things. First, it would give Barry an opportunity to develop patient, focused perseverance. In previous lifetimes, he'd gotten into the habit of not finishing what he started, which prevented him from developing his talents and certain virtues, such as patience, hard work, and endurance. Second, it would give Barry an opportunity to develop his inner life, which he'd avoided in previous lifetimes. He was someone who was always on the go, moving from one activity to the next, with little direction or thought given to the meaning of these activities in his life.

During his recovery, Barry had hour after hour to contemplate his predicament, to wonder, and to be still and listen. His condition forced him to become an observer of life. Now, as someone on the sidelines of life, he contemplated human nature and the human drama around him. He also began to recognize an aspect of himself that was beyond this drama, an aspect beyond his personality, body, emotions, or mind. This was the greatest gift of his disability, a rare treasure that few experience except in their latest incarnations.

Usually accidents like this are freely chosen by the soul as a means for growth. Between lifetimes, after examining the many options, an agreement about a specific plan is reached between the soul and the aspect of the self that remains after death. In this state, we don't have the fear and resistance to conditions that we do while we're in the body. Beyond death, we realize the beauty and perfection of life.

Accidents that aren't part of the soul's plan are rare because the soul can often waylay them or minimize their effects. By working through our unconscious and intuition, our soul can influence even minor choices, such as how quickly we turn, what direction we turn, and other responses that we or others might make in a critical situation. So it's usually not by chance that some people walk away from disasters while others don't. This doesn't mean that those who are injured or die deserve it. Injury or death is neither a punishment nor a reward. It merely suits or doesn't suit the soul's plan at that time.

CHAPTER 9
Murder and Suicide

Taking someone's life or our own is the most grievous offense against the Self. When life is lost, so are many opportunities. Killing someone interferes with free will in the most extreme way possible. It interrupts the individual's spiritual plan, making it necessary to begin life again and bypass other goals in order to heal. If it were possible to relive that life again, the loss might not be so great, but it never is. Those same circumstances can never be duplicated. The victim may have to wait many lifetimes before similar opportunities present themselves again.

Killing sets the murderer back too. The murderer will be required to make reparations to the victim and experience whatever is necessary to prevent the murderer from killing again. Karma encompasses both learning and atonement. As the stories that follow show, atonement can be made in many different ways besides directly to the victim.

Suicide and murder require different lessons and consequently different strategies for healing, or balancing. Suicide is a serious offense and slows our evolution significantly, although we even learn from this. Fortunately, because the fruitlessness of suicide is apparent once we're out of the body and the memory of this fruitlessness persists on a deep level when we are incarnate, we rarely commit suicide repeatedly.

We all have committed suicide because it's a natural response to pain in our earliest lifetimes, when we have few resources for dealing with life. More lately, suicide has become common in teenagers, who may be older souls but lack the maturity for coping with life and who may have fallen under negative influences. Certain drugs have also played a part in suicide among some older souls.

The stories that follow show how killing and being killed are healed and how we grow in love and compassion as a result.

MURDER

Case J

Arnold committed murder in one of his earliest incarnations, which isn't unusual. Most murders and suicides happen early in our evolution, before we have the compassion, understanding, and self-control to inhibit them. When older souls commit murder, it's often a reaction to violence and hatred they experienced in their childhood.

Arnold grew up in a normal family for the times and he wasn't treated harshly or neglected, but life was hard. He worked in the fields from sunup to sundown. Lacking the discipline or physical strength to manage this without resentment and anger, Arnold coped by drinking, which lowered his inhibitions and unleashed his anger. As a consequence, he often got into fights with others who were also acting out. One day, a fistfight turned into a knife fight, and Arnold's opponent lost his life. Due to a lack of law enforcement, Arnold's crime went unpunished, and so his behavior never changed.

In his next lifetime, he reincarnated as a female named Ellen. Ellen worked in the fields in addition to caring for her invalid parents, her husband, and her children. This was another lifetime of hard work with little reward, but being a female, she wasn't allowed to express her anger. She found other ways of dealing with her feelings, such as talking with others, which relieved her of feeling persecuted and helped her accept her lot in life. She also learned to find pleasure in some of her daily tasks, especially sewing, weaving, and knitting. She discovered she could make lovely clothing, which gave her a sense of fulfillment and pride.

Ellen's soul chose this situation for two reasons. First, it gave Ellen a chance to face circumstances similar to those in her former life and improve her way of dealing with them. Second, although neither her mother nor her father was her former victim, caring for them was a way of partially repaying the karmic debt from that lifetime. To make it easier, her soul chose warm and generous parents. This way, it was almost assured that Ellen would work off some of the debt as well as increase her ability to love and serve others.

For her next lifetime, her soul chose happier circumstances, again as a female. The goal was to continue to strengthen her capacity to love. For this, she needed to experience the goodness of life. She was born to a warm, loving family dedicated to the ministry. Her parents raised money for the poor, fed and sheltered the homeless, gave of themselves to their parishioners, and still had plenty of love left over for their three children.

Although she wasn't as evolved as her other siblings, her good qualities were brought out and enhanced by the loving people around her. Her beauty also made her more lovable. When it came time for her to marry, she chose someone with the same calling as her father's, which continued the pattern of service. During this lifetime, she grew in inner strength, love, and understanding.

Over these lifetimes, she became strong enough for the final test. At last, as a male, she would meet the individual she'd killed and try to make final amends. Although people aren't required to meet again in another lifetime to balance karmic debts like this one, many choose to. This will only be allowed if the victim consents to it, however. The victim has to be careful in making this choice because it's never certain that a balancing will go as planned. Sometimes the people involved only create further entanglements.

Let's backtrack a moment and chart the victim's course. If you recall, the victim had a problem with anger too. To correct this, several female lifetimes were chosen, as they were for the offender. One of these was a lifetime of ease, which allowed her to develop a talent and other resources. As we saw in the offender's story, a talent (making clothing) was useful in her healing as well. The soul often uses someone's talents to overcome his or her challenges. That's one reason we evolve more quickly in our later incarnations, when we have more talents, than in our earlier ones, when we have few.

At last the victim, Rose, and the offender, Jim, met. They fell in love at first sight at a dance. Soon after that, they were married. Although this may seem inconceivable, many marriages and other relationships are founded on a karmic debt. The souls of the individuals bring them together under the guise of romantic love and bind them until the debt is met or met as much as the circumstances allow. Although either individual can leave anytime, the "cosmic glue" between them is often compelling. They feel a sense of obligation, compulsion, attraction, and sometimes repulsion. To those involved in a karmic relationship, it often feels like being under a spell.

To continue, before long, Rose fell deathly ill. The test had arrived. Would Jim care for her in her hour of need? Was he a loving enough person to do that? Favoring this was the sense of obligation that is felt from a karmic debt. A karmic debt usually fosters love and commitment between two people. Through our karmic relationships, we learn the meaning of commitment, and our ability to love is strengthened through that commitment. This was true for Rose and Jim. Jim nurtured Rose unwaveringly until she recovered, and although they were no longer obligated to remain together for karmic reasons, they gladly did.

This story is not unusual; many soul mate relationships begin as karmic relationships. This story shows how even murder can lead to love. In case you haven't already guessed, love is the outcome of all of life's stories and the outcome of the next one too.

Case K

This is another story of murder. It took place in the earlier incarnations of both involved. Sam, who took Henry's life, did it out of fear because Henry was threatening him with a weapon.

This brings up some interesting questions. Just as our laws make some allowances for killing under these circumstances, we also might expect our souls to. From the standpoint of atonement, this murder would require less atonement than some. But from the soul's standpoint, the question isn't how heinous a crime is, but what lack of understanding caused the crime and what lessons are needed to correct it. To answer these questions, we need to look more closely at what happened and why.

Sam and Henry knew each other and considered themselves friends. Their disagreement was over some livestock that Sam presumably owed Henry. When Henry came to claim what he believed was his, Sam met his hostility with more of the same. A fight ensued and Henry was killed.

From their souls' perspective, their feelings when this happened are crucial. Sam had his wife and two children in mind when he defended himself. Although Sam had responded aggressively, it wasn't out of rage, as Henry had. So Sam's lesson wouldn't be about controlling his anger. Still, Sam had ended someone's life, so he needed to be impressed with the sanctity of life.

Sam chose to learn this dramatically by having his next lifetime cut short. He could have chosen a gentler but slower way to do this, but this way had its benefits. When that lifetime ended so abruptly, it was a great loss to everyone who loved him, even though this was part of his loved ones' plans too. Regardless of the pain—or maybe because of it—loss brings with it many opportunities for growth for everyone touched by it. The lesson being complete, he entered his next lifetime with more compassion and a contagious appreciation for life.

SUICIDE

Suicide happens for many reasons. Why it occurred is important in determining the lesson that will follow it. There are several reasons for suicide, among them are being overcome by feelings of hopelessness and other negativity, inadequate coping mechanisms and resources, fear of the future, and to escape from physical pain. Suicide also happens because people lack an understanding of life and death. If the truth were known about life and death, suicide wouldn't be seen as an option.

One way the soul teaches about life and death is through a near-death experience. People return from these experiences with an awareness of their own vastness and immortality and a greater understanding of the purpose of life. Following a near-death experience, life becomes more than a search for happiness; it becomes a gift whose value is deepened by every experience—even painful ones.

Near-death experiences are an antidote to suicide, but there are others. Religion is one. Young souls vulnerable to thoughts of suicide are often born into religious families. By discouraging suicide, religions encourage facing life. Some religions even teach that life is a school, but few religions provide an understanding that helps people embrace life no matter what life brings. Understanding is a basic human need. It counteracts hopelessness and fear and fosters acceptance and compassion. Understanding is the best antidote to suicide. This is illustrated by the next story.

Case L

Anna began her life in a prison. Her mother was incarcerated for a theft she didn't commit. At age two, Anna was placed with a foster family outside the prison walls in the hope that she would grow up normally. Those who raised her took good care of her, but no one offered her any spiritual understanding. No one taught her that there's more to life and to herself than the obvious. Although life may not depend on this understanding, the quality of life does.

As a result, Anna grew up with little sense of herself beyond whatever currently held her attention. Living without any spiritual understanding is like living with blinders on: You miss the big picture. This was true for Anna. When faced with a problem, her context for understanding it was so narrow that she couldn't see her options or the problem's potential for good. So out of desperation and ignorance, she took her life.

For her next lifetime, Anna's soul devised a plan that would introduce her spiritual nature to her. A religious family was chosen along with an astrology chart that encouraged a search for higher meaning (Sagittarius and Pisces). She was born to a devout family that believed that God resides within everyone.

Her first experience of her spiritual Self wouldn't be an earth-shattering or transcendent one. Instead, awareness of this grew slowly within her until one day she was struck by feelings of devotion. Next, she became aware of a peaceful place within herself. Having made these two important discoveries, she was on her way to accomplishing her life purpose. But there was more.

One day, while waiting on a street corner for a ride, her vision shifted and she saw that all life was connected. She saw energy streaming out of and connected to every other form. This lasted only a moment, but it would remain with her the rest of her life. In that brief moment, she knew that life was not as it seemed. She knew that behind ordinary reality was a far different one. And she knew that she was inseparable from the rest of life. For her, this was the birth of that mysterious thing called faith.

Experiences like these are given to each of us by our soul at various points in our evolution to bring about similar realizations. They form the basis of what we call faith. When she encountered difficulties in her next lifetime, she didn't consider suicide. Instead, she found that she had an inner strength—faith, which she could draw on to help her persevere and learn from her difficulties.

Case M

Betty, a young soul, had difficulty coping with even life's littlest challenges, such as getting up in the morning, fulfilling responsibilities, communicating needs, and getting along with family members. She attributed this to being different and assumed this meant she was special. Feeling special helped her cope with her daily difficulties. When she felt persecuted or unloved, she'd withdraw to her room and tell herself she was above it all. She indulged in elaborate fantasies about what her life would be like in the future.

As Betty matured, little changed. When she began working as a clerk in her father's store, she approached it like everything else. She arrived at work late and treated the customers badly. When she was reprimanded, she didn't care. She maintained that she was special and destined for something greater. She didn't realize that she was the one creating her future. She dreamed of a husband who would take her away from the drudgery of her life and provide for her every need.

One day Betty met the man of her dreams, or so she thought. She flirted with him, and he asked her for a date. Their evening together was romantic, he was mysterious, and she was completely charmed. They continued to see each other until one day he told her that he couldn't see her anymore because he was married. She was crushed. He was perfect for her! How could this happen to her! That night, she went home, took a knife to her wrist, and bled to death.

If she'd had more resources for dealing with this blow and not so much invested in fantasy with this man, she might have been able to grow from this experience. Several conclusions other than the one she chose were possible. She might have concluded that she couldn't count on others to improve her life or that she had to improve herself to attract the right man. Instead, she concluded that life wasn't worth living without this man.

In designing a plan for her next lifetime, Betty's soul considered this conclusion, other reasons for choosing suicide, and her level of development. This plan included circumstances that would encourage her to develop a talent, parents whose religious convictions prohibited suicide, and an astrology chart that would limit fantasy and promote realism and hard work (earth signs). Correcting her ill-conceived conclusion at death demanded a slightly more creative approach. Because she'd concluded that life wasn't worth living without this man, her soul would try to arrange a marriage to the man of her dreams so that she'd see that that wasn't the answer.

As expected, she was more practical in this lifetime. She took care of her responsibilities more willingly, but not without some resentment. This isn't surprising. Even though an astrology chart brings out certain tendencies, it can't make up for a lack of development.

As planned, she met, fell in love with, and married the man of her dreams. But not long after that, he started drinking and staying out all night. Sometimes he'd come home in a drunken stupor, wake her up, and beat her. After one of these nights, she decided that she'd had enough and left him.

This opened up new avenues for her. An elderly couple who wanted to share their home with someone in exchange for household tasks took her in. This allowed her to study art, an interest she'd wanted to pursue since she was a child. She did this while supporting herself with other kinds of jobs. Her self-sufficiency and the freedom to pursue her own interests made this lifetime a very fulfilling one.

It should be apparent from these stories that karma isn't about punishment. How painful a lesson is doesn't necessarily equate with the severity of a crime. This doesn't mean that someone who kills thousands of people won't suffer for it. The greater the transgression, the greater the atonement; and both learning and atonement often involve suffering. Furthermore, our evolutionary progress is slowed significantly by having to make amends, and having to live more lifetimes is punishment of a sort. But the most difficult aspect of karma may be the need to postpone our progress in other areas. Lifetimes dedicated to karmic debts are rarely as fulfilling as those dedicated to other goals.

CHAPTER 10
Unfortunate Love Affairs

When a love affair turns out painfully, it can affect our later relationships, including those in future lifetimes if the wounds are deep enough. Wounds deep enough to leave emotional scars lasting into other lifetimes are usually those in which abandonment, a loveless marriage, or infidelity has led to injury or death. This chapter examines how these experiences can be healed and their karma balanced.

ABANDONMENT

Case N

Juan and Maria married shortly after they met and immediately began a family. As can be expected, providing for their three young children was very stressful. Juan worked long hours, while Maria cared for the children. One day, Juan didn't come home. He returned the next day, without speaking, only to pick up some of his belongings. His father had abandoned his mother when he was a child, and now he was repeating the pattern. He probably never should have married or had children. It was contrary to his astrology chart, which was another reason he was so unhappy, although this is no excuse.

Abandonment is a serious offense, requiring atonement if it causes suffering. Mistakes like this are common with younger souls, who often fall out of alignment with their soul's plan. When that happens, the soul can usually improvise another plan. If Juan had remained with Maria, it would have been difficult, but he would have grown. Instead, he was led to a more satisfying life, one more in keeping with his plan, but he still incurred a karmic debt to those he'd abandoned.

Abandonment requires atonement when it causes hardship, as it did for Juan's wife and children. His children concluded that they weren't lovable, and Maria concluded she wasn't attractive or womanly enough to keep her husband. Although she never expressed these feelings, they kept her from pursuing another relationship. She concentrated on raising her children and being the best person she could be under the circumstances. Without a husband to support her, her life was very difficult

In her next lifetime, Maria's soul was anxious to get her involved in relationships again so that her growth wouldn't be stunted by avoiding them. For this, her soul chose an attractive appearance and an astrology chart that would increase her confidence and ensure opportunities for love. Her soul also arranged a meeting with someone she'd loved in a former lifetime with the intention that they would fall in love again.

Standing on the sidelines of love will never mend a broken heart. So when trust is an issue, the soul will make it as easy as possible to open up to love again. When she first met this man, she had reservations. She didn't trust him even though she had no reason not to. Eventually, his patience and their former love overcame her inhibitions.

The next story has a different ending. Sometimes the soul makes finding and maintaining a relationship difficult.

Case O

This story begins like the last, with a broken marriage and abandoned children. Like the husband in the last story, Thomas found the responsibilities of married life unbearable. He left because he wasn't able to support his wife and children and because he dreaded being tied down to a job. So Thomas took off with a goal of seeing the world and making money as he needed it. With no particular plan in mind, he let circumstances determine his course. When he met someone who needed a hand on a ship headed for another continent, he joined on.

Thomas hadn't gone far before he realized he'd made a mistake. He missed the comfort of his wife, Milly, and the smiling faces of their two children. He couldn't get them out of his mind and vowed to return to them as soon as he could. Unfortunately, that wouldn't be for months, and he couldn't get a message to them either. At least this gave him plenty of time to think about what he'd done.

When he arrived home, he was coolly received. During Thomas's absence, Milly had moved in with her parents, where she was supporting herself and their children by taking in laundry. Moreover, she had a new love and wanted nothing to do with Thomas. He was deeply hurt by this and determined to win her and his children back. One night while everyone was asleep, he stole into her room and tried to convince her to take him back. Her parents woke up and came in to see what the noise was all about. They chased Thomas out and threatened to have him arrested. This didn't stop him. He continued intruding on her in futile attempts to win her affection. Finally, she'd had enough and summoned the police, who jailed him for a short time. That only made Thomas more determined to have his wife or prevent anyone else from having her. In his desperation, he killed her and spent the remainder of his life behind bars.

In his next lifetime, he was born with a facial deformity, which inhibited his chances for romance. This challenge was intended to teach him the value of relationships (not having a relationship is one way of doing this). He spent this lifetime reading and helping other outcasts. He especially enjoyed his time at an orphanage, where he would hold the babies and play games with the older children. These children became his family, and his work with them enabled him to balance some of his karma.

In his next lifetime, he was the grandfather of the individual who'd been his wife. When he died, he left her a large sum of money. For several lifetimes following that one, he continued to donate time and money to helping children until his debt was fully paid. As a result, his compassion, love, and desire to serve grew.

LOVELESS MARRIAGES

Loveless marriages exist for many reasons, mostly for convenience and security. Some are arranged and some are just the result of poor choices. Loveless marriages are most common when religious or philosophical beliefs prohibit divorce or separation. Significant psychic injury can result from them if anger and resentment escalate toward hatred or violence.

Relationships serve many purposes spiritually, some of which can be fulfilled within a short period of time. Consequently, divorce sometimes serves our soul's plan more than staying together does. When that's the case, religious beliefs that prohibit divorce work against the highest good of those involved. On the other hand, prohibition of divorce is helpful when commitment is the lesson. Nevertheless, when commitment is forced, it often turns to anger and resentment. The value of commitment is never taught by forcing people to stay together, but through loving interactions. When people feel forced to stay together, marriages can become boiling pots of hatred and resentment. If this happens, the individuals may have to meet again in future lifetimes.

Case P

Sanjay and Roma married because their families arranged it. Although some arranged marriages are happy, this one wasn't. Roma wasn't attracted to her husband, who was nearly fifteen years her senior. Furthermore, Sanjay didn't understand her needs or see her as anything more than a possession. Although he was attracted to her and found her pleasant to be with, Sanjay and Roma didn't have enough in common to have anything more than a marriage of convenience. So Sanjay had liaisons with other women, which satisfied some of his other needs. But this wasn't an option for Roma. She felt her only recourse was death, since religious law forbade divorce. She chose suicide rather than stay in that marriage.

Roma reincarnated at a time and place where arranged marriages were a matter of course because those circumstances could further her lessons. The arranged marriage was part of her soul's plan. She had known her husband in a former lifetime and had had difficulty with him then. They chose before life to be together to learn to love and support each other in a committed relationship. The potential for deeper love existed, but they weren't able to open their hearts to each other. With time, they might have succeeded.

To balance the act of suicide, Roma's soul chose to try again with this same individual. This would give the husband another chance to learn to love her. It took nearly a century before an opportunity arose for them to be together again. This time, their souls made a loving relationship more likely by arranging that they be brother and sister. They had a satisfying relationship in that lifetime and went on to further their love in the following one as husband and wife.

The point is not that there should be arranged marriages, but that arranged marriages may serve to develop love for those who've avoided or ended relationships rather than persevered. This doesn't make arranged marriages right; they interfere with free will. But since they exist in our world, the soul uses them to bring about our lessons.

Case Q

Mukunda and Uma also had an arranged marriage, but one for the purpose of developing talents, not love. Unlike the previous couple, Mukunda's and Uma's lack of engagement with each other was useful to their growth. Their marriage provided Uma with financial support and time to develop her musical abilities and Mukunda with an opportunity to repay a karmic debt he owed to her. The arranged marriage served both of them for that lifetime, resulting in a satisfying partnership.

A loveless marriage doesn't have to end in bad feelings or injury. Sometimes these situations accommodate the needs of both souls. Whether a loveless marriage or infidelity leads to psychic damage or not depends on the choices of those involved. A loveless marriage or infidelity can cause damage lasting into future lifetimes if it leads to violence, death, or abandonment. The next story illustrates how infidelity can lead to karmic consequences. The story following that one illustrates a different outcome.

INFIDELITY

Case R

George and Amanda fell in love in their youth. As is usual with young love, neither understood themselves or their needs, but they married and began a family anyway. Before long, George became restless, feeling that something was missing in his life and that his wife and children were to blame. One day, without warning, George disappeared for a few days. He wanted to get away from his daily grind and be alone. Instead, he ran into some single friends who convinced him to go to a brothel with them. When he returned home, he had some explaining to do. George told Amanda that he'd discovered that the single life wasn't for him, which was true. Unfortunately, Amanda didn't believe him and began to feel insecure. She'd been betrayed in former lifetimes, so it wasn't surprising she felt distrustful despite his reassurances.

Amanda began looking through George's things and questioning his whereabouts. She also questioned her own attractiveness. One night she went out, presumably with friends, but ended up in a tavern where she met a man. They began meeting regularly and began an affair. When George followed Amanda one night and discovered her secret, he confronted her lover and they fought. Before anyone realized what was happening, George had delivered a deadly blow to his rival's head.

Needless to say, George would have to pay in this lifetime and several to come for not controlling his jealous temper. Amanda also suffered, for her lover's blood was on her hands too. She also lost a husband to provide for her and her children. This was a high price to pay for her indiscretion. Still, she needed more to ensure that this wouldn't happen again.

In her next lifetime she was raised in a small village where marriages were arranged and monogamy was the rule. This way of life wasn't questioned, and everyone made the best of the situation. She learned to do this too. Because infidelity wasn't tolerated, she no longer feared it and she learned to focus on values other than sexual attractiveness.

George had different lessons. First, he needed to learn to handle his jealousy and anger. Second, he needed to make atonement to the man he'd killed. And third, he needed to learn the value of commitment. To achieve these goals, his soul chose to be born into a wealthy and respectable family. His good fortune allowed him to act as a benefactor to the man he'd killed (which only partially atoned for this), and his upbringing taught him to handle his feelings in a socially acceptable way. His soul also arranged for him to fall in love with a religious woman, who was likely to remain faithful to him. This environment reduced the likelihood that anger and jealousy would be a problem because it lacked the frustrations common to poverty and provided the social constraints and values needed for a committed relationship.

It may seem odd that George's lessons were taught without pain or sacrifice. We're used to thinking of karma as punishment. The problem with looking at karma this way is that we might assume that those who are suffering deserve it because of something they did. This story shows the fallacy of this. As many saints have chosen challenging circumstances as sinners, and as many sinners are successful by society's standards as saints.

Case S

Brad and Carolyn knew each other in a former lifetime. In that lifetime, Brad had harmed Carolyn. In this one, he'd try to balance this karmic debt. The plan was simple: Brad would be born to a wealthy family, and Brad and Carolyn would fall in love and marry. This way, Brad would have the opportunity to repay Carolyn by supporting her in a comfortable lifestyle.

Brad and Carolyn married and lived comfortably for the first few years. Then, an unexpected misfortune hit the family, causing them to lose most of their money. After this, one bad financial decision after another compounded the stress on their marriage. Brad and Carolyn continued to grow apart as bitterness over their situation grew, each blaming the other for their problems.

Then, one day, Carolyn spent a seemingly innocent afternoon with a male friend, to whom she confided her troubles. They fell in love unexpectedly. Carolyn told Brad she was in love with another man and left Brad to be with him. Before long, Carolyn realized what she really wanted wasn't another marriage but time to discover who she was.

In this case, infidelity served a purpose. This couple had moved out of alignment with their plans, and the karmic debt owed to the wife couldn't be balanced under these new circumstances. Infidelity was the tool the soul used to end the karmic agreement and set both on new courses.

CHAPTER 11
Unfulfilled Potential

Many lead unfulfilling lives. An unfulfilling lifetime can affect our future lifetimes in several ways. For one, it can result in confusion about what we want, which can lead to another unfulfilling lifetime. If that happens, the soul will probably choose an astrology chart to try to break this cycle. A chart with a strong theme might be chosen, perhaps one with many planets in one sign. Such a chart narrows our focus and concentrates our energy, since the tendencies of that sign are difficult to ignore. Or, because the significant people in our lives have such a powerful influence on our attitudes and behavior, the soul might arrange for someone to give us direction or model decisiveness and initiative.

The most common result of several unfulfilling lifetimes is the belief that life is drudgery. This can become a self-fulfilling prophecy, leading to more unsatisfactory lifetimes. If we expect drudgery, we aren't likely to seek joy and fulfillment. Even though every life has some drudgery in it, if we're aligned with our soul's plan, we'll feel enlivened and excited about what lies ahead.

This joy and excitement is our soul's way of guiding us. Our soul also conveys our plan through our intuition, so learning to listen to and follow our intuition is necessary for fulfillment. This isn't always easy, however, because our intellect and conditioning often override our intuition.

We aren't born knowing how to use our intuition but learn this over many lifetimes by trial and error. We aren't born knowing how to find fulfillment either. Ironically, we learn this by first not being fulfilled. The suffering this causes makes us question what we're allowing to guide us—in failing, we learn to succeed. This paradox exists because the physical plane is a plane of polarities, which means that we learn about something by experiencing its opposite. We know what light is because we've experienced dark; we know joy because we've experienced pain. So no lifetime—even an unfulfilling one—is ever wasted.

Unfulfilled potentials also can cause us to distrust life and distrust ourselves in future lifetimes, resulting in bitterness and fatalism. Life is more difficult when we aren't living according to our soul's plan. This is because our soul will keep trying to bring us back to our plan. If we keep missing our soul's messages, more extreme methods will be used to get our attention.

Physical illness is just one way the soul shifts our attention from one thing to another. Another way is to introduce change, such as loss of employment, difficulties with a child or spouse, or financial loss. Life will always have its challenges, but our challenges will be fewer if we're aligned with our soul's plan. So the remedy for bitterness and fatalism is to become more aligned with our plan.

Many unfulfilled people find their way to therapists or healers, where they learn to get in touch with their feelings. This is often helpful because our soul uses our feelings to guide us, at least some of them. Feelings of depression, anger, sadness, and hopelessness often indicate that our needs—including our spiritual needs—aren't being met, while joy points us in a direction aligned with our soul.

Case T

Lucy was a slave for a family that had little concern for her as a human being. Because she had no freedom to make choices then, she didn't learn to make them. She was told what to do, when to do it, and how to do it. This childlike position made it impossible for her to develop the skills of an independent adult. So not only did Lucy have an unfulfilling life then because she was prevented from following her soul's plan, but she also didn't develop skills that would help her follow her plan in future lifetimes.

To counteract the effects of this experience, her soul chose a male incarnation next and an astrology chart and environment that would foster independence and initiative. Still, taking initiative and expressing feelings didn't come easily to him, although eventually he learned to do these things and he became a successful businessman. This lifetime balanced his lifetime as a slave, but the story doesn't end here.

In his next lifetime, he was born into a family dedicated to ending slavery. The plan was that he, now named Ben, would use the assertiveness he'd developed since his lifetime as a slave to further his family's cause. But life doesn't always go as planned. Ben felt uncomfortable with the issue of ending slavery, so he immersed himself in his business even though this wasn't particularly fulfilling.

Ben's soul had to find a way to draw out his compassion so that it could be used to fuel his life purpose. It did this by bringing a woman into his life who he'd loved in his lifetime as a slave. As his heart opened to her, he discovered his own sensitivity. His love for her activated his latent compassion and passion for the cause of slavery, which was also a passion of hers. This plan was only one of many possibilities. If Ben hadn't needed this woman's inspiration, he might never have met her.

Case U

This story is different. It's about someone who tried to find fulfillment but couldn't. Like many of us, he believed that fulfillment could be found in eating, drinking, and sex. He spent his life pursuing these pleasures, but in the end, he still felt empty and dissatisfied and died an unhappy, addicted man.

In his next lifetime, he still believed that happiness and fulfillment could be found by giving the ego what it wants. But this time, he indulged in different things. He concentrated on amassing material possessions and creating a comfortable lifestyle. Once again, he died feeling empty and unfulfilled.

In his next lifetime, he tried another tactic. This time, he denounced the ego's desires and turned to the priesthood in search of fulfillment. In serving others as a priest, he experienced more fulfillment and happiness than he ever had before. So for his next lifetime, he chose an astrology chart and environment that would deepen his motivation and ability to serve.

This series of lifetimes illustrattes how the soul often allows a natural course of learning to take place without stepping in to shape it. The soul honors free will, as it did in this story by allowing this individual to pursue his concept of fulfillment until he learned to choose more wisely.

This story is a reminder that fulfillment may be found only after many lifetimes without it. Fulfillment is usually found as a matter of course unless the vicious cycle mentioned earlier comes into play. If that happens, the soul may have to intervene. Although this cycle can usually be broken by selecting the right astrology chart and environment, sometimes more drastic measures are necessary. The next story describes such an instance.

Case V

This story begins with a lifetime of poverty and oppression. We all experience financial limitation at times in our evolution because it teaches certain lessons, but poverty can also simply be caused by our own choices. Lifetimes of financial limitation often lead to unfulfilling lifetimes because the oppression of poverty squelches the human spirit. When this happens, a sense of resignation and powerlessness might follow someone from one lifetime to the next until something intervenes. That's what happened to this individual. Feelings of resignation and powerlessness followed him into his next lifetime and then into another before his soul intervened.

This issue was finally addressed by choosing an assertive and ambitious astrology chart and an environment that allowed him freedom. This time, he was born into a white family in the

United States in recent years. If it had been a black family much before today, his feelings of powerlessness and resignation would probably have been culturally reinforced. But nothing in his environment gave him the message that he couldn't create the kind of life he wanted.

What happened was unexpected. Rather than behaving confidently and assertively, he continued to act as if he were oppressed and limited. Sometimes the chart and environment are just not enough to counteract the influence of many lifetimes.

To correct this, his soul arranged for him to win a large sum of money. Since money is equated with power in American culture, this gave him the confidence he needed. It also gave him the opportunity to develop his athletic skills, which furthered his self-confidence and sense of mastery. As he matured, he achieved other goals, which continued to reinforce his sense of power and control. If he'd failed in these endeavors, his soul might have introduced other means to build his confidence. So sometimes the soul brings good fortune into our lives regardless of merit if it serves our growth, as it did in this instance.

CHAPTER 12
Slavery and Servitude

Sometime during our evolution, usually in our earlier lifetimes, we have to endure slavery and servitude. These experiences are a necessary part of our evolution, teaching us compassion, loyalty, humility, selfless giving, and the importance of human rights. In fact, when our later life purposes involve service, numerous lifetimes of slavery or servitude are often chosen to develop our compassion and altruism. But just because slavery serves an evolutionary purpose doesn't excuse it. The oppressor has to come to realize the damage caused by inhibiting another's freedom.

Although slavery and oppression teach us valuable lessons, these experiences are damaging psychologically. They especially affect how we see ourselves in relation to others. Those who've had many lifetimes of slavery or servitude often feel inferior and form relationships that reinforce this. Their tendency to act subserviently is especially a problem in personal relationships because they often give too much or give inappropriately.

The experience of slavery can also result in feelings of powerlessness and hopelessness, which can attract further oppression, poverty, and servitude in subsequent lifetimes, thus creating a vicious cycle. In subsequent lifetimes, the oppressor is internalized and restrictions are created, not by an outsider, but by one's own limiting beliefs. Often, the soul has to intervene to break the cycle created by the repetition of these experiences. So slavery and servitude are combined in this chapter, not because they are the same, but because lifetimes of servitude often follow lifetimes of slavery.

Case W

This is the story of someone who had several lifetimes as a slave and a servant. When it came time to serve in less subservient ways, low self-esteem, the result of his earlier experiences, interfered with his feeling fulfilled in his work. The more he gave, the worse he felt about himself. In order for him to serve more joyfully, this would have to change.

The circumstances his soul chose to build his self-esteem were what you might expect: He was born into a wealthy and powerful family. Although he was somewhat uncomfortable with the power he had, this lifetime built his self-esteem, clarified the meaning of service for him, and showed him he was capable of leadership.

These arrangements don't always work out so neatly, however. Sometimes those who've been servants for many lifetimes don't overcome their sense of inferiority so easily. When this happens, their evolution is slowed while time is taken to balance this. Some may even decide to pursue other avenues of growth instead of returning to the path of service. Regardless, these initial lifetimes of service teach many valuable lessons. Let's go back and see what was learned from this individual's experiences with slavery.

In his first lifetime as a slave, he was treated badly by his owner. He was bought to do hard physical labor, and his master was determined to get his money's worth. But even though he was treated like an animal, he knew better. To him, this cruelty proved his master, not himself, to be the animal—or worse. Despite this harsh treatment, he retained his sense of pride and learned that social class isn't the measure of a human being.

In his next lifetime, he chose slavery again, with a goal of helping other slaves retain their pride amidst their oppression. He was able to serve as a model for this because of his astrology chart and two previous lifetimes of mental illness, which developed his compassion and understanding.

Other experiences of servitude continued to build his compassion and understanding. These lifetimes also motivated him to serve, not a master, but as a teacher for the oppressed. Serving an ungrateful and cruel master doesn't increase our desire to serve, but it can build our compassion to the point that humanitarian service becomes compelling.

The next story of slavery is different because the girl in this story didn't have the same degree of understanding to bring to her experience of slavery. Our first experience of slavery usually occurs in our early lifetimes when the lessons of slavery are most pertinent and before we have much understanding. Slavery provides a vehicle for learning some of our most basic lessons. Many older souls also choose this experience for their own reasons, as another story will show.

When young souls experience slavery, their initial reaction

usually is to agree with their oppressor's assessment of them. Just as children take a parent's word for who they are and what they can do, younger souls believe what others say about them. Realizing we aren't inferior is a big step in mastering the lessons of slavery. This realization may come during our first experience of slavery or several lifetimes of slavery later. When it does come, it signals our readiness to move beyond this experience if we choose to. As we saw in the last story, some choose to remain slaves for a time to either help the enslaved or heighten their own compassion and drive to serve. The next story describes what most of us experience before we're ready to move on to other lessons.

Case X

Karinna was born into conditions of slavery. Although she lived with her family, her interactions with her parents were limited by their long working hours and their exhaustion. Her parents would take her along with them into the fields where she would occupy herself with whatever was available. She grew up this way, having little experience with the world or how others lived. She never saw the more luxurious homes of the wealthy because the rich lived some distance from their small enclave of huts, although she heard stories of their comforts and wealth.

When the overseers came to collect the little that Karinna's community had to show for their labors, the laborers were verbally abused and spat on. It didn't take long before Karinna began to believe that she and her family were being punished for being who they were. Clearly, some people were favored over others, and her religious beliefs led her to believe that the fortunate were better people than the unfortunate. Her family didn't contradict these ideas with assertions of injustice or criticism of the wealthy. Rather, they looked to their oppressors as gods who had the power to bestow happiness on them if they proved themselves worthy. This attitude isn't typical of all slaves, but it is typical of younger souls caught in slavery.

One day, a man appeared on horseback. He had come some distance to deliver a proclamation. It stated that Karinna's community was no longer bound to a certain individual but to someone else. As a result, they would have to hand over a greater portion of their produce than before. Needless to say, this was a great hardship for their community. Some of the younger men talked of protesting by holding back some of what was due, but what would that mean? For one, it would mean they were worthy of making a decision like this, an idea unacceptable to some. After all, who were they to question their rulers?

Karinna had just become old enough to marry when this happened, and she had some ideas of her own. Her fear was that if her community rebelled, the strongest and bravest of her small community would have to answer for it. She didn't want to see anyone hurt. She'd suffered all her life and she would suffer some more, but the disruption of her community was more than she was willing to risk. However, her opinion mattered little and her worst fears came to pass. The man she most wanted to marry was taken and jailed. Karinna died several years later, ending this hard, lonely life.

In another lifetime, she reincarnated as a male slave named Harvey, who worked in the stables of a wealthy landowner.

Harvey was reliable, trustworthy, and content. He had no desire to improve his lot in life nor did he see any opportunity to. Then, one day, another stableman was taken on who had traveled the world with his former master. As they worked, Harvey heard tales of places he'd never even imagined existed and began to long for his freedom. The new stableman also told Harvey of an underground network where slaves could be taken safely to freedom. This gave rise to a plan, which won them the freedom they longed for.

Karinna's experience of slavery taught her some basic lessons. She learned to work hard and attend to responsibilities necessary to survival. Our early lifetimes often revolve around survival. From our struggle with survival, we learn patience, perseverance, and basic physical skills. From humbling conditions, we learn humility. In being powerless, we learn to be receptive, accepting, and appreciative of the little things in life. Through service to others, we learn to be loyal, to obey, and to follow orders. These aren't minor accomplishments, although most of us take them for granted. Because most of us are no longer in our earliest incarnations, it may be hard for us to appreciate the importance of these lessons. Nevertheless, our current capabilities stem from these early lifetimes of struggle with survival.

By the next lifetime of slavery, as Harvey the stableman, he had sufficient mastery over these basic lessons to graduate from slavery once he realized the injustice of it, but he needed help coming to this realization. His previous experience of slavery, as Karinna, had taught him that rebellion wasn't wise when he, as

Karinna, lost a lover to imprisonment for rebellion. To help Harvey break free of slavery, his soul arranged for him to meet an adventuresome, freedom-loving individual. If Harvey hadn't been ready to move beyond slavery, he probably wouldn't have met this liberator.

It would be naive to assume that this individual was unscathed by these experiences of slavery. It took several lifetimes with strong (fiery) astrology charts to overcome the passivity that had developed from these lifetimes of slavery. Charts and circumstances were also chosen to build relationship skills and eliminate subservient behavior. This individual had had little experience with intimate relationships before the two lifetimes of slavery, and those lifetimes were spent virtually alone. He needed practice forming equal partnerships.

Case Y

Unlike the last story, this one involves a very evolved soul who chose to experience slavery to advance his spiritual goals and improve the human condition. This individual had already experienced many lifetimes of slavery, servitude, and other forms of oppression, which had developed his appreciation of life and the blessedness of every human being.

As a result of these lifetimes, this individual learned to transform feelings of hatred, anger, resignation, and fear into compassion and understanding. He also developed an uncanny ability to intuit the feelings and inclinations of others. This may seem like an unlikely talent, but those who are oppressed learn to read their oppressors as a way of protecting themselves. They become astute observers of human nature and learn to manipulate it to ensure their safety. This is one reason that those who've had many female lifetimes are sensitive and insightful. Sensitivity was an invaluable outgrowth of this individual's many lifetimes of oppression. Now he was prepared to enter into other oppressed circumstances, not to further his sensitivity, but to use his gifts for the good of all.

Around age eighteen, he was captured and taken on a boat to a faraway country. While traveling to this distant land, he was kept in shackles and fed a minimum of food until the food ran out. After that, he became very weak and unable to perform the work expected of him. He was beaten for his lack of productivity and left to mend.

In the delirium that followed, he had a vision of a distant and beautiful land, where rolling hills stretched for miles. He floated over this land, surveying it as if in flight, floating and gliding peacefully over its verdant hills. Suddenly, he saw something that grabbed at his very being. There below him were people, like himself, laboring under the threat of a whip in the fields of this beautiful land. He saw himself among them, disheveled and stooped with exhaustion. At that moment a voice spoke to him saying, "Be at peace. Someday you will save your people from this oppression. When the time comes, you will be guided." From that point on, he began to recover from his fever despite not having food for several more days.

As foretold, the next few years were filled with sweat and exhaustion, but he never forgot the powerful message of this vision. One day as he lay on his mat on the floor, a figure of light appeared to him. It didn't speak, but it projected a mental picture of a rebellion with himself as its leader. Like a movie, it unfolded a plan for a rebellion in detail, showing him how he could lead others to freedom. It even indicated when this plan should be carried out. When the time came, he acted with the certainty and vision needed to inspire the confidence of others and lead them to freedom.

Although he suffered, no healing was needed in future lifetimes. He was strong enough to live through this with no lingering psychological damage. This is not only because he was victorious, but also because he knew he was more than a slave throughout this trying experience.

The vision had helped to crystallize his sense of purpose, but his many lifetimes also had taught him that great powers lay within him and gave him confidence that good would prevail. This set him apart from many of the others, but he's no more special than any of us. He just had reached a point in his evolution, as we all do, when he was ready to give back to humanity what he'd learned from his many incarnations. Most of the world's greatest accomplishments have come from people like him who've developed their talents, understanding, and desire to serve over many lifetimes of arduous lessons.

CHAPTER 13
Mental Illness and Mental Disability

Mental illness and mental disability (or mental retardation, as it was once called) are being addressed in the same chapter because they often deliver similar lessons. But mental illness isn't always a pre-life choice and mental disability nearly always is. These conditions also evoke similar responses from others, with abuse being familiar to both.

    Mental illness and mental disability have existed in every culture throughout history. Both are necessary to our evolution because of what they have to teach us, both as individuals and as a society. Compassion for those who are helpless is the most obvious teaching, but not the only one. The dependency of these conditions also teaches us the value of independence and freedom.

    Because these conditions create a drive for freedom, an experience of mental illness or mental disability may be useful when a drive for freedom and independence is lacking, as is common in our early lifetimes. In these lifetimes, we may become too comfortable in our dependency and afraid of venturing out on our own. If it seems like we won't choose to be more independent and self-sufficient when the time comes for that, then mental illness or mental disability might be chosen to create a drive for independence.

Just because most of us experience mental illness and mental disability in our early lifetimes doesn't mean that everyone who's mentally ill or mentally disabled is a young soul. Older souls choose these conditions too. Just as someone who's mastered the lessons of slavery might choose to experience slavery again to help those who are enslaved, many older souls choose mental illness or mental disability to help the afflicted make the best of this experience or to teach their caretakers important lessons.

We all know of mentally ill or mentally disabled people who've taught their caretakers priceless lessons about love, compassion, acceptance, patience, and endurance. It's obvious that those who are mentally ill or mentally disabled aren't just learning lessons; they are also our teachers. If we can open our hearts to what they have to teach us, these unusual people can enrich us immensely.

The stories that follow illustrate how mental illness and mental disability can advance our evolution and why these experiences are sometimes chosen by older souls.

MENTAL ILLNESS

Case Z

Hanna suffered from schizophrenia in times when it was treated as possession. Because the townspeople thought Hanna was possessed by evil, she was feared and punished. Her soul chose this illness to accelerate her evolution, knowing that that choice at that place in time was likely to lead to abuse. Hanna was an older soul who was capable of handling abuse and using it for her growth, but the same might not have been true of a younger soul. For this reason, very young souls are rarely put in potentially abusive situations. Usually, when younger souls are abused, it's not part of their plan.

At first Hanna was jailed in unbearable conditions, but when it became a burden to continue to care for her, her oppressors found a way to justify her death. They said that because she was a witch, she had to be burned to put an end to her sorcery. With great ceremony and self-righteousness, they burned her in the town square for all to see. This ended Hanna's life at the age of twenty.

Although this was a short life, it was a significant one. As all suffering does, it taught Hanna compassion. It also taught her to accept life and her lack of control of it. Her surrender gave rise to a new awareness, a new state of consciousness. As a result, in her next lifetime, she was able to remain detached from the ups and downs of life, centered amidst life's storms. She had learned what those who spend hours a day meditating learn—that she was not her body, her mind, or her emotions; she was Spirit. This short lifetime of persecution had prepared her to bring her Light into the world and to serve in a way that most are incapable of serving until their very last lifetimes.

Case AA

Monica is a very young soul, who is alive today, who chose schizophrenia to increase her compassion and appreciation for the value of independence. Because Monica doesn't have Hanna's inner resources and inner strength, Monica's soul chose to be born into a supportive and understanding environment. Monica has been cared for at home under the supervision of a psychiatrist. In our modern times, Monica's had the advantages that medication can bring to this illness, allowing her to lead a relatively normal, although sheltered, existence.

It hasn't been possible for Monica to learn the same lessons as Hanna because Monica is a much younger soul. Nevertheless, Monica has learned some fundamental lessons, and this situation has also provided her with a safe environment in which to learn about a highly technological and complex world. Ordinarily, such a young soul would have reincarnated into a simpler society, where expectations of accomplishment are minimal and the basics of survival are taught patiently by family members. In Monica's case, the schizophrenic lifestyle provided this kind of support and training amidst a technological society.

We have to wonder why Monica chose to be born into a technological society at all. Besides her own learning, the reason was that she had something to teach her caretakers. Her mental illness arrested her family's busy, materialistic lifestyle long enough to make them look inside themselves. Schizophrenia, like any personal crisis, was a way of advancing the spiritual and emotional growth of her family members. This illness not only demanded her parents' patience, but allowed them to appreciate the depth of love they have for their daughter and for each other. Monica's mental illness brought her family closer together and enhanced their ability to give to each other. These are not minor accomplishments but significant landmarks in our evolutionary journey.

Case BB

This story differs from the last two because the mental illness in this story was not a pre-life choice but a means for coping with an intolerable situation. When grossly abused or traumatized, younger souls often retreat from the world by becoming mentally ill. Although these individuals may not consciously choose to be mentally ill, they give up on life, and it takes this form. This choice is like suicide in its intent to escape life, but the individual remains alive while abdicating the privilege of living consciously and deliberately. Ironically, this tendency to surrender their will together with their inexperience is what makes young souls vulnerable to abuse in the first place.

Melissa was sexually abused by her father until she escaped by leaving home. While she was on her own, she was repeatedly raped by an acquaintance. After this, she stopped participating in reality and became a ward of the state. The soul is rarely responsible for circumstances that create this much stress on someone so vulnerable. When this happens, the soul's plan has usually gone awry because of others. Although the soul will do what it can to right such a situation, sometimes it's not enough.

It might be interesting to look at how the souls of those involved tried to influence this situation. First, Melissa's soul hadn't anticipated that her father would be abusive. Since he hadn't been abusive for many lifetimes, he wasn't a likely perpetrator. When his intentions became apparent, his soul attempted to prevent the abuse by trying to influence him and others involved intuitively. When this didn't work, Melissa's soul created an illness that required medical intervention in the hope that the physician would discover the abuse, but the physician wasn't thorough enough. Their souls even brought another woman into the picture to deflect the father's interest, but to no avail.

Sexual abuse is addictive and difficult to stop once it begins. Their souls could not reach Melissa's mother either because she was involved in her own addiction with alcohol. This, too, was unexpected. Melissa's mother was a sensitive woman, capable of lovingly caring for her daughter. She began drinking when she miscarried her second child. Although the miscarriage was part of the mother's soul's plan, it wasn't anticipated that she would turn this tragedy into another one by coping with it this way.

Addiction is damaging not only socially, physically, and emotionally, but also spiritually. It's one of the most common reasons for plans going awry, although many people turn to addictions *because* they are out of harmony with their soul's plan. Because addictions interfere with receiving the soul's messages, many who are ruled by their addictions find themselves trapped in unfulfilling lives. Even more tragic is when an addiction interferes with other people's plans, as it did in this case. Then, some future balancing might be needed, not to punish the addict, but to show the addict the importance of taking charge of his or her life and not spoiling the lives of others.

Although Melissa's mental illness eventually did bring Melissa the protection she needed and some increase in compassion, it prevented her from accomplishing her other lessons. Unfortunately, when the order of our lessons is changed, the same understandings aren't necessarily achieved. Since mental illness wasn't part of Melissa's plan, she didn't benefit from this experience like those in the previous stories had.

Since this is a present-day story, Melissa's future lifetimes are yet to be written. Melissa's future plan is likely to include a nurturing environment, one that will help her rebuild her confidence, sense of self, and trust. She's likely to choose a small town or village in which to be raised, where her safety can be better assured, and a fiery astrology chart for ego development and assertiveness. She will also need to learn to cope with the stress of life in other ways than by escaping.

Since Melissa's mother never made the connection between Melissa's mental illness and her own lack of responsibility, the mother's future healing will undoubtedly include an experience that will help her realize the damage caused by addiction. The circumstances for this lesson shouldn't be hard to arrange because she'll be predisposed to alcoholism and likely to become alcoholic again. Because addictions continue into future lifetimes, the lessons of addiction are unavoidable.

The mother's healing is also likely to entail a situation similar to her miscarriage to help her gain the spiritual understanding she missed by drowning her sorrows in alcohol. For instance, this might be accomplished by having someone close to her lose a child. With an astrology chart that fosters soul-searching (Sagittarius or Scorpio) and people who could give her the proper guidance, her chances for finding answers to the questions she formerly avoided would be good.

As for the father, a variety of issues will need to be

addressed. One of them is power because incest involves an abuse of power and will. Another is self-restraint, especially as it applies to thoughts, since the father's fantasies played a key role in the abuse. And the last is empathy.

Because empathy is learned by being victimized, karma that teaches empathy often looks punitive. But learning empathy is part of everyone's evolution. No one escapes this lesson, although some people have fewer experiences of victimization than others because they learn faster. This is one instance in which the father is likely to need to be victimized in the same way his daughter was. Empathy can't be taught any other way. So his future victimization will be a consequence of—not a punishment for—abusing his daughter. Please don't conclude from this that victims deserve their suffering.

Correct use of power is usually taught by meeting the negative consequences of abusing power. The father might be taught this lesson with an astrology chart that emphasizes power (Scorpio), one that could set him up for a fall. Or, the soul might arrange circumstances in which he experiences an abuse of someone else's power.

As for developing greater sexual restraint, the father's soul might choose an environment for his next lifetime as devoid of sexual stimulation as possible, perhaps a culture with many sexual taboos or one that de-emphasizes sex. Several lifetimes in an environment such as this might be needed to balance his habit of sexual fantasy and indulgence.

MENTAL DISABILITY

The last two stories are about mental disability, or retardation. Mental disability is nearly always a pre-life choice and something we all experience, usually in our earlier incarnations. Intellectual limitations serve many lessons. Besides patience and compassion for those less skilled, mental disability teaches us to live moment by moment. Someone who's limited intellectually is unable to think abstractly or consider the past or future. Their world consists only of the present. In this way, they're similar to very young children or other living creatures.

Learning to be in the moment is by no means an insignificant lesson. It's central to our later lifetimes, when we learn to transcend the personal self. The ego is the aspect of the personal self that delights in projecting itself into the future and ruminating about the past. The ego keeps us from experiencing ourselves in the present, the only place where we can know our divine Self. This truth is known to meditators, who meditate to transcend the ego and experience their true nature. Because it can teach us to be in the moment, mental disability is sometimes chosen by Old souls who want to learn to do this.

Case CC

This is the story of a very young soul named Jeanne, who chose to experience a mild mental disability for shelter and protection from the world. Because very young souls don't have the resources or coping mechanisms for dealing with the outside world, many very young souls grow up in small villages, rural settings, institutions, or other places that provide them with the safety they need while helping them learn the basics of survival.

Jeanne was mentally disabled in a society that usually cared for such people in institutions. But Jeanne was only mildly disabled and could benefit from schooling, so she was placed in a special school and looked after by her parents. She flourished in this environment, which provided her with what she needed for her physical and emotional well-being.

Jeanne's situation was ideal, but why do many mentally disabled people find themselves in situations that aren't ideal? One answer is that sometimes the environment doesn't fulfill the soul's expectations. Because the choices of others can't be controlled, the environment doesn't always turn out as the soul intended. Another reason is that older souls might choose mental disability under difficult conditions to accelerate their growth or learn a certain lesson. Very young souls never choose a potentially abusive or neglectful situation, however, because they don't have the inner resources to benefit from it.

Those who are damaged by the experience of mental disability are usually very young souls whose environment has become abusive or neglectful despite the soul's intent to the contrary. In these instances, those who've contributed to the neglect or abuse will face lessons to make sure they won't continue doing this, while the victim will need a protective environment to mend.

Because very young souls are so vulnerable, abusive situations in early lifetimes can be devastating, requiring many lifetimes of simple living and protection to heal. Needless to say, this is a real loss to their progress. Many of them spend lifetimes

Mental Illness and Mental Disability

in an institution or some other sheltered environment where they are cared for and their trust is rebuilt.

On the other hand, institutionalization has often been the culprit, fostering the same abuse and neglect from which some individuals are recovering. Institutions serve both those who are learning greater compassion for the neglected and abused and those recovering from neglect and abuse. Good institutions and bad ones have always existed, and the soul will use both to serve these two different purposes.

Case DD

The Old soul in this story had several monastic lifetimes before a lifetime of mental disability. Because of the stifling effect of monasticism on individuality and intimate relationships, his social development and initiative were inhibited. Although his monastic lifetimes advanced him spiritually, they left other aspects of himself undeveloped. Having finally reached a point in his evolution when a devotional lifestyle was no longer beneficial, he needed other experiences to help him become more well-rounded. So he chose to experience mental disability.

In that lifetime, he was profoundly mentally disabled and born into a large, close-knit family. This situation served several purposes. He was able to learn vicariously from this even though he was unable to process information consciously. His observations about family life and relationships were recorded by his unconscious and would be available to him in later lifetimes. In addition, the forced passivity aroused his desire to act on life, which balanced his former tendency to be passive. Except under such extreme circumstances, this couldn't have been achieved so quickly. And finally, it strengthened his desire to serve children and others who are helpless.

CHAPTER 14
Imprisonment and Seclusion

Extensive imprisonment or seclusion invariably leaves a mark, especially if those conditions are forced and inescapable. Even when someone chooses to be cloistered away, this experience, although valuable in some respects, usually requires future balancing. One reason is that human relations, which are an integral part of life, don't exist under these conditions nor does sexuality in the fullest sense. Both imprisonment and seclusion foster habits that are usually unproductive to future relationships, as we will see in the stories that follow.

Nevertheless, imprisonment and seclusion are universal experiences from which we can benefit if we have the inner resources to grow from these experiences. Imprisonment and seclusion can increase our appreciation for life and its small pleasures, much like poverty can. When the ego's pleasures are stripped away, as they often are in these situations, all that's left is the Self—if we can get beyond our desires for what we don't have.

As might be expected, older souls are more capable than younger souls of using these kinds of limitations for their growth. While imprisonment can be enlightening for an Old soul, it can be devastating to a very young one, so the soul avoids placing very young souls in circumstances that could lead to imprisonment. Seclusion, on the other hand, holds some potential for growth even for the youngest of souls.

Unfortunately, those who imprison others don't discriminate between young souls and old souls. Imprisonment often happens to vast numbers of people at once, most of whom do not have this as part of their soul's plan. For those whose plans are disrupted, their evolution for lifetimes to come is affected. As for those responsible for this, they'll have to realize and atone for the damage they've caused.

The following stories depict the positive and negative effects of imprisonment and seclusion. But please understand that just because imprisonment may work for good and be part of someone's plan does not condone it. It's never in someone's soul's plan to victimize someone else even if it is part of the other's plan to be victimized. Rather, the soul will put an intended victim in a situation with this potential without knowing exactly who will carry out the injustice, if anyone.

IMPRISONMENT

Case EE

Phillip was a prisoner of war. He was tortured, maligned, and left with nothing to eat or drink. When he finally succumbed to death, he'd been left alone for over a week. This is an instance of gross injustice, regardless of what justification his oppressors might have had. If Phillip had been lacking in compassion, this experience might have resulted in hatred lasting for lifetimes.

However, Phillip was able to accept this injustice without needing to avenge it.

Hatred is undeniably the most damaging consequence of experiences like these. For a very young soul, the pain of such an experience may be translated into fear, mistrust, and hatred lasting for lifetimes. So those who've reaped hatred from such experiences need nurturing in their next lifetime.

Phillip didn't enter his next lifetime with hatred, but there were other negative effects. After this cruel treatment, Phillip didn't have the same trust and optimism as before. His will to live was affected too, which was important to balance. Without the will to live, we're likely to waste our life or go through it without the appreciation that life deserves.

To balance this, in his next lifetime, his soul intended to show him the goodness of life. It selected a loving family and an astrology chart that would foster courage, confidence, and a zest for life (Leo). This was to be a fun and interesting lifetime, full of exploration and growth. Unfortunately, he didn't benefit from these circumstances as he might have because he had difficulty enjoying himself when others were suffering. So in his next lifetime (the current one), his soul shifted his energy toward service. He now works as a missionary, which gives him plenty of opportunities to express his compassion. After this lifetime, he will probably be ready for different lessons.

This analysis wouldn't be complete without also examining what his oppressors needed to balance their actions. What caused them to mistreat someone like this? The answer will determine what will be needed to balance these actions. Since this particular injustice was spawned by religious beliefs, the balancing would be accomplished by instilling religious tolerance. To do this, astrology charts that promote tolerance (Aquarius, Sagittarius, Gemini, and Libra) and conditions that teach this were selected.

This was accomplished for one individual by having him reincarnate into a small town where conformity was expected and religious intolerance was widespread. He was born into a family that was scorned by the community because they didn't worship like the rest of the town. When he grew up, he was determined to find a more accepting environment, only to wind up in a similar situation elsewhere. This caused him to examine his own values and why people felt and behaved the way they did. Eventually he moved to a large city, where he met people who were more broadminded. There, he expressed his opinions about religious intolerance with the same fervor he'd expressed his religious views in his previous lifetime. At least this time, his opinions didn't hurt others or infringe on their rights.

He was unusual in how quickly he learned his lesson. Not everyone involved in the incarceration and torture learned so quickly. Another individual, a woman in her next lifetime, was born into similar circumstances but with entirely different results. She responded to the townspeople's scorn by accepting it as a just evaluation of herself and by treating others with the same disdain. She died unhappy and alone and with no more understanding than she'd come in with. It took two more lifetimes of similar circumstances before she began to appreciate our basic right to differ with each other.

The first individual suffered little in balancing the grievous acts of his former lifetime because he learned so quickly. The second individual wasn't as fortunate, taking three precious lifetimes to learn the same lesson. Clearly, when we're receptive to learning our lessons, karma doesn't have to be so painful. Only when we resist our lessons, more painful experiences might be introduced to get our attention. Both individuals, of course, were also required to make amends to the victim in addition to changing their attitudes and behavior.

Case FF

Bill was jailed for a crime he didn't commit. It was a serious crime, and he was sentenced to life in prison. Bill didn't accept incarceration. He couldn't let go of his anger and resentment. These feelings festered, absorbing energy that could have been used more productively. Because those who sentenced Bill believed they were serving justice, their future lesson, if any, might entail improving the criminal justice system.

Bill's reaction is understandable. One of the problems with the criminal justice system is that it doesn't give prisoners enough hope or incentive for change. Destroying our hope for a better future undermines our will to live. Under these conditions, anyone would find it difficult to overcome despair and grow, let alone the young souls who fill most prisons. Younger souls in this position are likely to remain angry and resentful, which is only likely to lead to more violence in the future. So although incarceration may succeed in punishing a criminal act and in taking criminals off the streets, incarceration often does nothing to redirect or transform anger and little to prevent the act from happening again.

For his next lifetime, he needed a productive outlet for his feelings of anger and injustice. If he were to become a lawyer, he could be a watchdog for similar injustices. Arranging this wouldn't be difficult, since he would already be inclined toward this. A suitable astrology chart, the right family, and certain opportunities were arranged to attract him to that profession.

He did become a lawyer, but he quit before long because he felt overburdened by the legal profession's procedures. So this individual's healing would have to wait for another time, which isn't unusual. Lessons are often put off and others taken up. Nevertheless, he did gain from his unjust incarceration, if only an appreciation for the plight of those unjustly accused. No one understands this like someone who's experienced it.

Case GG

Todd was also incarcerated for a crime he didn't commit, but Todd's attitude was different than Bill's. This could be attributed to his astrology chart and past-life experiences, particularly a lifetime as a judge. What he learned from that lifetime was that, regardless of its imperfections, the law serves society as best it can. This belief was deeply held and helped him accept his incarceration.

Once he accepted being incarcerated, he put his energy into making the best of it. He took advantage of the prison's meager educational opportunities and studied law. He got together with other prisoners and read through cases, examining the intricacies of each one and envisioning how they were tried. This led to many fruitful philosophical and ethical discussions.

This story turned out differently from the last one because incarceration was part of Todd's plan, while incarceration wasn't part of Bill's plan. Todd's incarceration served to both focus his energies on the law, a former topic of interest, and uplift others. Despite the unusual setting, Todd was performing just the service his soul had set out to do, so no healing or balancing would be needed.

Any challenge that is part of our soul's plan will be easier to handle than a challenge that's outside it. If the challenge is part of our plan, an astrology chart and an early environment will have been chosen to help us grow and learn from that challenge. If not, our astrology chart, environment, and past-life experiences may even work against growing from that challenge.

SECLUSION

Case HH

Tuku grew up in a remote part of the world with just a small tribe to call his family. Although he wasn't unhappy, he was intent on living apart from even this small band of people. There comes a time in everyone's evolution when the life of a hermit is appropriate and beneficial. For Tuku, the choice to live apart was clear and right.

Seclusion can be beneficial because it teaches self-sufficiency, responsibility, practicality, and independence. In being secluded from others and from society, we meet the consequences of our choices directly, with no one else to lean on or blame. This kind of lifestyle is particularly helpful for fairly young souls because it forces them to rely on themselves and develop their survival skills.

If someone would benefit from seclusion, but he or she is too complacent to choose it, the soul might arrange it. Younger souls are especially apt to become complacent, accepting the help of others even when they can provide for themselves and others. When this happens, the soul might arrange a shipwreck, a natural disaster, a war, or other circumstance to force the individual to become more independent.

Tuku took easily to seclusion since he had experience with it. In his previous lifetime, he'd been forced to care for himself when his parents died and left him to tend to their land and livestock. During that lifetime, he didn't have an opportunity to socialize or marry. This balanced a former pattern of dependency that had become unhealthy.

After several lifetimes of dependency and then seclusion, Tuku lacked social skills, and his next lifetimes would have to focus on developing those skills. The danger of not following lifetimes of seclusion with lifetimes of relationship is that we may lose interest in relationships altogether. Relationship may come to feel too foreign and demanding, making avoidance more attractive than engagement. Once this pattern is established, it can be difficult to break.

Case II

This is the story of someone who continued to lead fairly secluded lifetimes despite his soul's efforts to the contrary. Even lifetimes as a woman didn't dissuade him from avoiding companionship. Apparently, his lifetimes of solitude were rewarding, and he saw no reason to live with others. Only after many lifetimes alone did he finally have an experience that proved to him the importance of relationship.

One day, he found himself trapped in a snowdrift, unable to move. Someone with a dog, who was seeking people who might have been trapped by the storm, found him. Because he needed several weeks of care, a neighbor came by regularly to attend him. He was so touched by her kindness that he vowed to do the same for someone else sometime. It wasn't enough anymore just to take care of himself. His soul had finally gotten through to him; and the energy of his astrology chart, which fostered service and relationship, was activated.

He had two more lifetimes of service with some involvement in relationships, but his relationships lacked intimacy. He cared for others but didn't allow them to care for him. By shunning dependence, he closed the door to greater intimacy. Despite his soul's efforts to create experiences of intimacy, he remained aloof from his partners.

Even though he didn't master the lessons of intimacy, he gained enough understanding about relationships from these lifetimes to be allowed to choose a lifetime apart from intimate relationships. This time, he chose to be a priest, where he could serve without being intimate. As long as he can continue to grow through such choices without inhibiting his progress in other ways, he will probably be allowed to. But sometime he'll have to face the lessons of intimacy again and master them, since they are part of everyone's evolution.

CHAPTER 15
Conclusion

We have seen that all our experiences—or lack of them—color our psychology and behavior. We are unique composites of everything we've ever experienced. All our previous experiences and all the astrology charts we've ever had influence our psychology in a given lifetime. This is obvious with twins, who have nearly identical charts but different ways of responding to the energies of those charts. Even identical twins aren't clones of each other. This is because they bring to the expression of their charts everything they've learned in former lifetimes. Once we understand this, we can appreciate the personality for what it is: a vehicle for evolution.

The task of evolution is not to do away with the personality. Evolution uses the personality to learn the lessons of this reality. But in our later lifetimes, we establish a different relationship to our personality: Instead of the ego expressing itself through the personality, the divine Self expresses itself through the personality. This shift doesn't come about violently through our own efforts or will, but naturally and gradually in the course of our evolution. Meditation and awareness can hasten this natural process. The Kingdom of God is not won by force, but by mastering the personality's lessons. We evolve by learning to express our personality positively.

Since our personality is the vehicle for our evolution, we need to understand it and use it for our growth. The astrology chart is the best tool I know of for understanding the personality. The chart pictures the personality, with the signs representing personality traits, such as timidity, humility, passivity, tenacity, assertiveness, creativity, sensitivity, objectivity, reliability, vivaciousness, courage, helpfulness, friendliness, unconventionality, compassion, and perseverance, to name a few. Once you have a sense of your personality and its traits, as described in your astrology chart, then ask yourself why these traits are part of your life now. A trait is part of your personality for one of four reasons:

1. You chose that trait to help you accomplish your life purpose. For example, Aries, which confers independence and courage, might be chosen if your life purpose requires leadership.

2. You chose that trait to balance a destructive pattern established in a former lifetime, possibly due to a trauma. For example, Leo gives courage, which could neutralize a fear of something.

3. That trait was developed and ingrained through repetition in past lives. For example, you might be very meticulous even without any Virgo in your astrology chart because meticulousness (a Virgo trait) was practiced or required in many of your lifetimes.

4. You are learning the lessons that accompany that trait. The twelve signs represent the lessons necessary to our evolution. When the time comes for a certain lesson, we're born under the appropriate sign. For example, if we're learning patience, we may be born under Taurus, which gives patience and steadfastness.

There comes a time late in our evolution when we've mastered our basic lessons and balanced most of our karma and all that remains are minor refinements of our lessons. Then, it's time for us to contribute our wisdom and talents to humanity in some form of service. How we choose to serve depends on our past experiences and the preferences and talents we've developed. Some individuals serve by inventing or discovering things, while others serve by producing beautiful works of art or happy children. We all have something to offer when the time comes. But just as we have to learn the lessons of childhood before we can function as an adult, we have to master the basic lessons before we can contribute to the world as fully as possible.

We're here not only to learn our lessons and develop our talents, but also to help others do the same. Whether we realize it or not, the universe uses us to bring about other people's lessons. We are all deeply interconnected and intimately valuable to each other's plans. Everyone's lessons touch the lives of many, each in a different way. Greta, who was stirred into service by the plight of her paralyzed friend, was touched as much by the lesson of being paralyzed as her friend.

This is why we have to be so careful not to interfere with

someone else's plan. Doing so disrupts the entire web of lessons connected to that person. You can't remove anyone from the web of life without it affecting many others. Yet we have the power to do this.

How different the world would be if we didn't interfere with the plans of others! There still would be difficult lessons, but we would have the right chart and environment for learning them. Life is made more difficult and tragic by having the freedom to harm others. The paradox is that we learn and evolve largely through free will, so we wouldn't want to do away with free will. But our lives and the lives of others would be vastly improved if only we knew how to use our will better.

It's easy to blame God for the injustices around us—poverty, disease, and death—without fully appreciating the role that our choices play. Much of the sorrow in the world wouldn't exist if we made sounder, more compassionate choices. What we call evil is often the result of uninformed and unenlightened choices. As long as some people on this planet are still learning the basic lessons of life, there will be evil. Still, this doesn't absolve us from our duty to help those less informed or enlightened.

One opportunity for helping people is through the criminal justice system, which is failing miserably. Just as our religions need to shift their focus from retribution, so do our prisons. Before we can do this, we'll have to agree that humankind is innately good. If we believe that some people are born evil, we'll treat them inhumanely, and they won't heal. No one is born evil, but many are born with a great deal of fear and a lack of wisdom, which can result in evil actions, especially when compounded by abuse or neglect.

Do we solve this problem by putting people in prisons where many are further abused? Imprisonment might serve many valid purposes, but healing isn't one of them. Criminals are as much in need of healing as victims. Unless their healing is addressed, hatred and violence are likely to continue. The tragedy of the criminal justice system is that we don't help this population, which is so much in need of our help. We've seen how the soul heals people by providing a nurturing environment and role models and opportunities to develop some talent or skill to build self-esteem. We know these ingredients are healing—we apply them in healing the victims. Why is it so hard to see that criminals need the same help as part of their rehabilitation?

Fear of our own dark side causes us to treat criminals as if they were subhuman or as if their ignorance and imperfections were contagious. Fear is at the root of our treatment of them, just as it is at the root of their treatment of others. This fear prevents us from feeling the compassion that all human beings deserve. How can we claim to be worthy of being their wardens when we can't do it compassionately? They might not deserve freedom, but they do deserve our compassion and help. As it is, our treatment of them heaps more injury on them, only delaying the healing that could be begun.

The Law of Karma doesn't punish; it heals and teaches. The hope in presenting these stories is that they will inspire people to work toward improving our world by teaching and caring for others. Many people in this world need healing. Even if healing can't be completed in this lifetime, it can at least be begun. No love is ever lost on someone regardless of how it may seem. We have to believe this and carry on humanely and compassionately toward everyone. We have to treat everyone as we would like to be treated.

The seed of our divinity is within us even in our earliest incarnations. We are never really separate from the Divine. Our souls are always present, trying to guide us throughout our evolution. But in our earliest lifetimes, we function primarily from our egos and have more difficulty responding to our soul's guidance. So younger souls especially need the help of older, wiser souls. It is our responsibility to do what we can to help all people. Ultimately, any improvement we make in the lives of others will also improve our own.

Fortunately, our lifetimes on the physical plane eventually lead to greater love and compassion. This compassion is often taught through the experience of victimization. At some time, everyone has been a victim and everyone has been a perpetrator. These two roles are two sides of the same coin, which teaches compassion. This compassion underlies the service that is the hallmark of our later incarnations.

Nevertheless, if our physical incarnations were all there is, our suffering might be difficult to justify, just as suffering is difficult to understand within the context of just one life. But in light of our entire existence, this suffering is a small price to pay for the wisdom and understanding we gain. The physical plane is like a school, preparing us for an eternity of growth and service in nonphysical realms. The wisdom, love, and understanding we gain from our physical incarnations will be used to serve the Divine and all creation. Our service, then, will be not only to physical systems like our own, but also to nonphysical systems of reality.

Within the Great Plan, each of us is uniquely important and equally significant. Furthermore, we are mutually dependent on and irredeemably intertwined with each other. Ignorance of this truth doesn't diminish it. The recognition of this comes by opening our hearts to the possibility that within each of us lies a spark of divinity that unites us all. Once we become open to this truth, we can't help but discover it.

Despite how it may seem, we are not long on this earth. Our physical incarnations are infinitesimally brief within the scheme of our existence. But within the Great Plan, these lifetimes are infinitely precious, laying the foundation for all that lies ahead. We are blessed with the gift of life, but we have to make it what it can be. We may have no choice about existing or evolving, but we have every choice in how we will do this. Let us carry on with faith in our purpose and determination to act in the highest good of all.

ABOUT THE AUTHOR

Gina Lake is a spiritual teacher and the author of numerous books about awakening to one's true nature, including *Trusting Life, Embracing the Now, Radical Happiness, Living in the Now, Return to Essence, Loving in the Moment, What About Now? Anatomy of Desire,* and *Getting Free.* She is also a gifted intuitive with a master's degree in counseling psychology and over twenty years experience supporting people in their spiritual growth. Her website offers information about her books, free e-books, book excerpts, a monthly newsletter, a blog, and audio and video recordings:

www.radicalhappiness.com

Books by Gina Lake

(Available in paperback, Kindle, and other e-book formats.)

Embracing the Now: Finding Peace and Happiness in What Is. The Now—this moment—is the true source of happiness and peace and the key to living a fulfilled and meaningful life. *Embracing the Now* is a collection of essays that can serve as daily reminders of the deepest truths. Full of clear insight and wisdom, *Embracing the Now* explains how the mind keeps us from being in the moment, how to move into the Now and stay there, and what living from the Now is like. It also explains how to overcome stumbling blocks to being in the Now, such as fears, doubts, misunderstandings, judgments, distrust of life, desires, and other conditioned ideas that are behind human suffering.

Radical Happiness: A Guide to Awakening provides the keys to experiencing the happiness that is ever-present and not dependent on circumstances. This happiness doesn't come from getting what you want, but from wanting what is here now. It comes from realizing that who you think you are is not who you really are. This is a radical perspective! *Radical Happiness* describes the nature of the egoic state of consciousness and how it interferes with happiness, what awakening and enlightenment are, and how to live in the world after awakening.

Trusting Life: Overcoming the Fear and Beliefs That Block Peace and Happiness. Fear and distrust keep us from living the life we were meant to live, and they are the greatest hurdles to seeing the truth about life—that it is good, abundant, supportive, and potentially joyous. *Trusting Life* is a deep exploration into the mystery of who we are, why we suffer, why we don't trust life, and how to become more trusting. It offers evidence that life is trustworthy and tools for overcoming the fear and beliefs that keep us from falling in love with life.

Loving in the Moment: Moving from Ego to Essence in Relationships. Having a truly meaningful relationship requires choosing love over your conditioning, that is, your ideas, fantasies, desires, images, and beliefs. *Loving in the Moment* describes how to move beyond conditioning, judgment, anger, romantic illusions, and differences to the experience of love and Oneness with another. It explains how to drop into the core of your Being, where Oneness and love exist, and be with others from there.

Anatomy of Desire: How to Be Happy Even When You Don't Get What You Want will help you discriminate between your Heart's desires and the ego's and to relate to the ego's desires in a way that reduces suffering and increases joy. By pointing out the myths about desire that keep us tied to our ego's desires and the suffering they cause, *Anatomy of Desire* will help you be happy regardless of your desires and whether you are attaining them. So it is also about spiritual freedom, or liberation, which comes from following the Heart, our deepest desires, instead of the ego's desires. It is about becoming a lover of life rather than a desirer.

Return to Essence: How to Be in the Flow and Fulfill Your Life's Purpose describes how to get into the flow and stay there and how to live life from there. Being in the flow and not being in the flow are two very different states. One is dominated by the ego-driven mind, which is the cause of suffering, while the other is the domain of Essence, the Divine within each of us. You are meant to live in the flow. The flow is the experience of Essence—your true self—as it lives life through you and fulfills its purpose for this life.

Living in the Now: How to Live as the Spiritual Being That You Are. The 99 essays in *Living in the Now* will help you realize your true nature and live as that. They answer many question raised by the spiritual search and offer wisdom on subjects such as fear, anger, happiness, aging, boredom, desire, patience, faith, forgiveness, acceptance, love, commitment, hope, purpose, meaning, meditation, being present, emotions, trusting life, trusting your Heart, and many other deep subjects. These essays will help you become more conscious, present, happy, loving, grateful, at peace, and fulfilled. Each essay stands on its own and can be used for daily contemplation.

Getting Free: How to Move Beyond Conditioning and Be Happy. Freedom from your conditioning is possible, but the mind is a formidable opponent to freedom. To be free requires a new way of thinking or, rather, not thinking. To a large extent, healing our conditioning involves changing our relationship to our mind and discovering who we really are. *Getting Free* will help you do that. It will also help you reprogram your mind; clear negative thoughts and self-images; use meditation, prayer, forgiveness, and gratitude; work with spiritual forces to assist healing and clear negativity; and heal entrenched issues from the past.

What About Now? Reminders for Being in the Moment. The secret to happiness is moving out of the mind and learning to delight in each moment. In *What About Now*, you will find over 150 quotes from Gina Lake's books—*Radical Happiness, Embracing the Now, Loving in the Moment, Living in the Now*, and others—that will inspire and enable you to be more present. These empowering quotes will wake you up out of your ordinary consciousness and help you live with more love, contentment, gratitude, and awe.

For more info, please visit the "Books" page at
http://www.radicalhappiness.com